JUSTIFICATION:
BY GRACE THROUGH FAITH

Edward W. H. Vick

'Not faith but grace is the cause of justification, because God alone is the cause. Faith is the receiving act, and this act is itself a gift of grace. Therefore one should dispense completely with the phrase 'justification by faith' and replace it by the formula 'justification by grace through faith.' — Paul Tillich

Energion Publications
Gonzalez, Florida
2022

Copyright © 2022, Edward W. H. Vick

Unmarked Scripture quotations are translated or adapted by the author.

Scripture quotations marked RSV are from the Revised Standard Version of the Bible, copyright © 1946, 1952, and 1971 National Council of the Churches of Christ in the United States of America. Used by permission. All rights reserved worldwide.

Scripture quotations marked NEB are taken from the New English Bible, copyright © Cambridge University Press and Oxford University Press 1961, 1970. All rights reserved.

Title Page Quote: Paul Tillich, *Systematic Theology. Vol. III*, Chicago: University of Chicago Press, 1959, p. 224

ISBN: 978-1-63199-785-3
eISBN: 978-1-63199-786-0

Energion Publications
P. O. Box 841
Gonzalez, Florida 32560

energion.com
pubs@energion.com

Table of Contents

Foreword..vii

I INTRODUCTION..1
    Centralities and expression   1
    Importance of the subject   2

II FAITH THE STARTING POINT..3
    Witness   4
    The irreducibility of faith   5
    Provision and acceptance   7
    Faith and reason   9

III THE RIGHTEOUSNESS OF GOD......................................13
    The availability of God   13
    Old Testament teaching   14
    Grace   15

IV THE KNOWLEDGE OF GOD..17
    God is made known in Jesus Christ   17
    Revelation: the basis of theological discussion   18
    Faith is of God   19
    The righteousness of God:
        significance of the term   19
    The meaning of the term 'righteous'   20
    Distinction between ethical and religious
        conceptions of righteousness   22
    The prophets' view of sin.   23
    Paul   24

V THE GRACE OF GOD 27
- Grace is free — 27
- Grace as gift — 28
- The sovereignty of God's grace — 30
- Grace and faith — 30
- Augustine and Pelagius on grace — 32
- Thomas Aquinas on grace — 34
- The analogy of faith — 36
- Parables of grace — 37

VI JESUS CHRIST: THE OBJECT OF FAITH 39
- Personal disclosure — 39
- Disclosure and response — 41
- Proclamation, *kerygma* — 45
- God known only to faith — 48
- What Scripture teaches about the knowledge of God — 50
- Judgment and salvation — 52

VII FAITH 55
- Faith and the Spirit — 55
- A preliminary denial — 57
- What faith is not — 57
- Distortions of faith — 59
- No word, no faith — 62
- What faith is — 63
- Old Testament teaching — 64
- Faith in the New Testament — 66

VIII 'BY FAITH ALONE' 71
- The meaning of the expression — 71
- Many other things — 71
- Paul's statement — 72
- Luther's statement — 73

IX JUSTIFICATION 77
Relationship with God	77
Vocabulary	77
Fiducia and other terms	78
The church and the covenant	78
Christus pro nobis, Christus in nobis	**79**
Justification and the judgment of sin	80
'Counted righteous' or 'made righteous'?	82
The alternatives?	82
A legal fiction?	83
Simul justus et peccator	88
The eschatological element in justification	92
'Righteousness of God' in Luther	93
What Luther reacted against	94
Summary 98	

X THE WORKS OF FAITH 99
'Acts' and 'Works'	100
Excursus on Galatians	100
Bonhoeffer: Discipleship is not 'cheap grace'	103
Obedience 104	

XI SANCTIFICATION 107
Summary statement	107
Sanctification	107
Walking 108	
Original sin	109
Sin in the Old Testament	110
Reckoning?	114
Sanctification and sin	114
Paul, Wesley, Schleiermacher	115
Sanctification not absolute perfection	116
The New Testament paradox	117

XII FAITH, FREEDOM AND WORKS 121
    The state of faith   121
    Death imagery   122
    Faith, freedom, works and law   124
    James and Paul on works and faith   131

XIII ALL IS OF GOD 135
    Faith and church   135
    'All is of God'   137
    Assurance 139

Foreword

It was always my concern to speak about faith in Jesus Christ. I have done that in various ways.

This document represents the content of a course I gave during my days at the Theological Seminary of Andrews University, entitled *Righteousness by Faith*. It was very well received, and I am now happy to put the content of that course into some shape with a minimum of change. I have done so without making serious alterations to the content of the course as given. So it is not a 'book' in the sense that it has had all the (I hope not too frequent) repetitions ironed out. Let's then call it a 'writing'! When one is teaching it is sometimes advisable to engage in a judicious amount of repetition. For repetition is the mother of memory. It can also be the father of indifference. Hence the repetition must be judicious. Moreover one can repeat while approaching materials from a different angle, as is in evidence here. Nor have I revised and revised the materials as I would have done if I wanted it to achieve the status of a 'book'. I believe that it is suggestive and useful simply by being what it is — a transcription (largely) of the spoken words in front of a group of students. What I have done is to provide frequent headings, so that the materials can be easily found and recognised.

It was an introductory course. That means that some topics were not dealt with in any great depth and others were only briefly mentioned. One of these is the problem of faith and history. I have dealt with this topic in my book *History and Christian Faith*,[1] which writing deals with the essential issues. It is short and concise.

---

1   Edward W. H. Vick, *History and Christian Faith*. Nottingham: Evening Publications, 2003

I hope that it might very profitably be read to complement what is contained in this writing, and serve as an introduction to the issues involved and also serve to guide to the literature on the subject.

Another writing of a complementary nature to this writing I have called *A Little Book About Faith*.[2] Topics are treated here as they have not been treated in the same way in the other two writings. All together (I think) the three make a good trio.

---

2   Available in typescript.

I INTRODUCTION

Centralities and Expression

We can get many things straight if the few things gotten straight at the outset are central enough. So it is important to recognise what is central and to come to grips with it. The recognition of what we have made centralities is often a painful process, for they are of course taken for granted. It is essential to get the right things at the centre, to lay good foundations.

The preacher's task is to set before the church and the world the witness to an accomplished fact — that the human being finds its centre and life, its meaningfulness in Jesus Christ. That can be said in many different ways. It can be said wrongly and distorted so that, with all good intentions, the way it is being said blurs and even obliterates the essential matter.

There are two particular problems for the theologian and the preacher: to know what the central things are and then to speak of them in a way that makes contact with the hearer. In other words, we must get our theology straight — and that is a big enough task, but not the biggest one. Then, we must prepare the idioms through which the essential message is to be conveyed. We have lived in the twentieth century and now are in the twenty-first. It has been a time of unprecedented revolution. So some reassessment of the forms of our presentation has become urgent. There is a message and there is the demand for its interpretation. We have the heavenly treasure in earthen vessels. We employ human speech, expressions, forms of thought. These are the human means through which the essence has to be conveyed. These forms of expression may change. We need not feel that theological language is sacrosanct. The expressions hallowed to memory and stamped in the church's life in the bygone centuries of her witness, in creed, and theology may have to be radically revised to meet the needs of our contemporary world. However true a thing is, if its truth or relevance is not seen, there's not much point to preaching it that way. So we must have courage for reexamination. Forms of expression can clarify. They can also confuse. We must (need it be said?) prefer lucidity and perspicuity to imperspicuity and obfuscation. The West is not predominantly Christian. Rather it is secular and both unsophisticated and sophisticated in its secularity.

So, in light of such basic challenges, we must ask two questions: What does it mean to be a Christian? How best can I give expression to the essential fact: that salvation is in Jesus Christ acknowledged as Lord? In this course we shall be doing both things at once: Clarifying the essential and searching for adequate means of expression for today, as well as examining ways of expression of the past. Remember: neither yesterday's piety nor forms of expression are adequate to today's need.

Importance of the Subject

'Righteousness by faith' is a concise way of saying that human salvation is in God alone, that God has moved to man and has been received by him. The expression does not say everything about salvation. It is important in that when properly understood, it excludes certain wrong ways of expressing an understanding of man's salvation, for example

that man is the source of his own salvation (against legalism and Pelagianism in all their forms);

that faith is the source of salvation (against fideism).

Note that if the expression is not read aright it could give a very wrong impression. We must look at the implications of the expression in order to know what it means. So it will help if we set before us the nature of the problems involved, if we set out what the expression 'righteousness by faith' might be taken to mean.

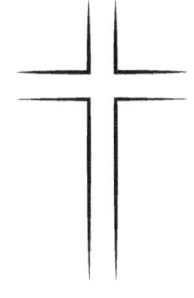

II FAITH THE STARTING POINT

The starting point must be with the fact that we believe. Since this is a theological treatment, we cannot tarry with any other questions which might on other occasions be raised relative to the existence of faith. We believe. That is the basic datum. 'I believe in God ... Jesus Christ ..., etc.' For a theological treatment of the meaning of life and cosmos, we must start here. We believe. I believe. In the context of our commitment, we ask the meaning of that commitment. That is, our thinking about the Christian religion begins from within. It begins with the accomplished fact of redemption in Jesus Christ. It begins there but it does not end there.

Thus primarily the only thing that can be said and done is, to witness. Theology roots in witness. What has been accomplished in us has been effected indeed through certain agencies. It provides us with a subject matter to discuss and explain, to expound, to have contradicted, to have to defend. But at the root there is this fact of faith, which at least for us cannot be contradicted and cannot be further explained. It is a surd. We may be driven back from theological outposts to inner theological defences, but when the citadel is reached we shall find it to be the home of faith alone. We will say later that there is no faith without God, that to say faith is to say God. What we are now insisting upon is that whenever we are pressed to declare what is the essential matter of Christianity we are driven back to the certainty of faith. And to be driven to faith means to be driven to witness.

Witness

That is how it was in the New Testament. The emphasis on the character of the apostolic declarations as testimony, as witness is inescapable in the Biblical literature. It is interesting that the English term 'martyr' is reserved for the supreme act of witness, even to death for the sake of the faith. In Greek, all Christians were *martures*. So *I John* 1:1–3: the testimony to the revelation of life in Jesus Christ creates Christian *koinonia*, fellowship. The work of the apostle Paul is frequently characterised as *marturein* (witness) e.g. to the Jews at Corinth. *Acts* 18:5; in recapitulating his labours in Asia he speaks similarly, '*testifying* both to Jews and to Greeks of repentance to God and of faith in our Lord Jesus Christ'. *Acts* 20:21, cf. verse 24. He is encouraged by the vision and the voice. 'Take courage, for as you have testified about me at Jerusalem, so you must bear witness also at Rome' *Acts* 23:11. So with the earliest apostolic preaching: e.g. *Acts* 8:25.

The witnessing was to an accomplished fact, which is expressed in two ways in the New Testament. On the one hand, there is the confession of the presence of faith, and on the other of the activity of God which created this faith. The groundwork is thus laid for a twofold treatment of the basic fact, 'I believe.' God's activity in Jesus Christ is the possibility of faith. If we are clear we might use the terms 'subjective' and 'objective' of the two aspects. But we will be well advised to avoid these terms if they are unclear.

The expression occurring with great frequency in the New Testament is *pisteuo eis* plus the accusative. The object of faith is now the Son (*ton huion*) Do you believe in the Son of God (*John* 9:35); now 'him' (*auton*) i.e. Jesus, e.g. *John* 20:31: 'Many believed on him there'; now 'me' (*eme*) e.g. *John* 10:37,38: 'If I am not doing the works of the Father, then do not believe me'; now 'God', e.g. 'He rejoiced with all his household that he had believed in God (note the perfect tense)' *Acts* 16:34. The object of faith is now 'the

Lord' (*toi kurioi*) (*Acts* 18:8); now 'the Lord Jesus. *Acts* 16:31. 'And they said, Believe on the Lord Jesus and you will be saved, you and your household; now 'him' (*ep' autoi*) 'He who believes in him will not be put to shame' *Romans* 9:33.

The verb 'to believe' is also used in the absolute, i.e. without an object, as in the following instances: 'He said, Lord I believe.' *John* 9:38; 'But many of those who heard the Word believed.' *Acts* 4:4. 'Many of them therefore believed.' *Acts* 17:12; 'But some men joined him and believed' verse 34; '… the gospel … is the power of God to every one who has faith' *Romans* 1:16. It was the conviction of the writer of the Fourth Gospel that the witness to faith's presence had something to do with the participation in faith on the part of the hearer. So, 'these are written that you may believe that Jesus is the Christ, the Son of God, and that believing you might have life in his name'. *John* 20:31.

THE IRREDUCIBILITY OF FAITH

That faith is irreducible has been recognised by many theologians, in many different traditions. It has been presented in various ways in the context of different theologies. We are here concerned only to stress this element of finality or irreducibility about faith. It will then be important to define the meaning of faith. It is important to be aware that not every employment of the term 'faith' points to the same phenomenon. For example, Thomas (13th century) and Aulen (20th century) use the same term, but how different is the reality to which they point. We are at present concerned with the finality of the appeal to faith.

To what is it that a final appeal is to be made? What is it without which the appeal to the authority of Scripture or of church would be empty? For obviously the authority of Scripture or of church rests upon and is accepted on the basis of some precedent authority, without which it would not have the authority it has. The reason why not everybody allows the authority of Scripture is that not everyone has faith. The authority of Scripture is no problem to the believer. Faith opens the way to its acknowledgment. The absence of faith means that such authority is closed. That faith has acknowledged such authority does not entail that there will be agreement about how that authority will be defined. That is for theology to determine and express.

We have here been concerned with the centrality and irreducibility of faith. We must seek later to define its meaning, since some of the meanings it has been given have been unfortunate and misleading, for example when it is defined as assent, or solely in terms of feeling, or as an independent human work (a denial of the principle which the expression 'righteousness by faith' attempts to state.)

To take one example of many statements insisting on the irreducibility of faith:

> 'Faith is an elemental energy of the soul, and the surprise that we are undergoing at not being able to bring it under direct observation is only an echo of the familiar shock with which we learn that science has ransacked the entire bodily fabric of man, and has nowhere come across his soul; or has searched the heavens through and through with its telescope, and has seen no God. If anyone were to ask 'What is it you mean by thinking, or loving, or willing?' who could tell him? It would be obviously impossible to explain, except to a being who could think, will, and love.
>
> And faith stands with these primary intuitions. It is deeper and more elemental than them all: and, therefore, still less than they can it admit of translation into other conditions than its own; — can still less submit itself to public observation. It can never be looked at from without. It can be known only from within itself. Belief is only intelligible by believing. Just as a man who is asked to say what love is, apart from all its outward manifestations and results, must be driven back on the iteration —'Love is — what love is everyone who loves, knows. No-one who does not love can ever know;' just as a man, who is challenged to describe and define his feelings or his desires, when stripped of all the outward evidences that they can possibly give of themselves, is thrown into inartic-

ulate bewilderment, and can give no intelligible answer, and can fashion to himself no distinct feature or character, and can only assert, confusedly, that he feels what he feels, and that to desire is to desire: so with faith.'[3]

PROVISION AND ACCEPTANCE

The distinctiveness of the Christian religion is that it relates faith intrinsically to Jesus of Nazareth. Jesus is the Christ. It is by faith that Jesus is acknowledged to be the Christ. We say this at the outset to indicate two necessary ways of approaching our subject. We are speaking about both God and man when we speak of faith, and of righteousness by faith. Man's faith is not of his own creation, out of resources native to his humanity. All gifts are from God, including the faith which is the instrument through which those gifts come. The one who responds to God's love in faith knows that that love was a reality before he knows its depths.

There are two ways of approaching this reality. One is to talk of God's grace. The other is to talk of man's faith. The ground of faith is in God's grace. The reality of faith is the reconciliation in human experience. This is not a dichotomy. We ought never to set the objective and the subjective in opposition. That would produce a host of theological problems to be avoided at the outset. We must therefore say, holding both aspects together: what man is, is based upon what God has done. What God has done is with a view to what man may become. Some ways of speaking of God have no relevance for faith, i.e. those with no reference to the activity of God in Jesus Christ, and in the Spirit in the church. Word and Spirit must be held together.

Paul's central message in the book of *Galatians*, which involves a sharp rebuke to the members of the church, is that if one adds something to Jesus Christ one has turned away from God. What is added makes no difference, even if it is added in the name of God and of Jesus Christ. So Paul's amazement and concern is based

---

3   Charles Gore, D.D., *Lux Mundi*, London, John Murray, 1904, pp. 5,6

upon his recollection of the past experience of the Galatians. They had turned from the bondage of the legalism of paganism to the freedom of Jesus Christ. But now they are turning to the bondage of a new legalism in the name of Jesus Christ. They are turning back again' (4:9.) Faith refers beyond itself to God. Works lead us to turn in upon ourselves. Thus an inversion of perspective takes place. That is what had happened in Galatia. Paul is disappointed, frustrated, and baffled.

We may put the point by indicating the classical theological distinction between a doctrine of atonement and a doctrine of salvation. We use these terms technically of a subject matter treated differently. If we say that the subject matter of the Christian religion is God's act of grace in Jesus Christ through which man comes to salvation, we may thus talk both of the activity of God in Jesus Christ, and also the activity of God in the person who comes to believe in Jesus Christ. God provides. The human receives. It is unfortunate that the distinction between these ways of approach which should be complementary, but with the priority on God's gracious activity, should have been transformed into a dichotomy. We must hold both together the provision and the appropriation. There is no faith and no salvation if Jesus be not crucified and risen. There is no meaning to cross and resurrection if he who died and was raised is not believed in. If we might so speak, the fact of the Christ and the faith of the believer must always be held together. If they are not aberrations of various kinds result.

The following chart sets out the two aspects, but needs careful explanation. For example, we must not oppose and radically contrast 'history' with 'faith'. (For further explanation of this see my book *History and Christian Faith*.) It would be a useful exercise for the reader to attempt a careful explanation of the contrasts made here and come to a conclusion about the relationships.

Provision	Acceptance
Objective	Subjective
Atonement	Salvation
Christus pro nobis = Christ for us	*Christus in nobis* = Christ in us
Word	Spirit
History	Faith

The believers are to bear witness both that God has acted to save in Jesus Christ; and that they have faith, that they have been reconciled to God in Jesus Christ.

Faith and Reason

Theology is concerned with faith. An ancient definition says that theology is *fides quaerens intellectum* — faith seeking understanding. Theology does not create its materials out of whole cloth. Rather it finds its data to hand in the believing Christian, and in the believing church. Theology is an attempt to expound with care and with precision and with a degree of comprehensiveness the implications of faith. Theology attempts to give as adequate an explanation as possible of the fact of faith. This means that myriad questions spring forward for an answer. Given the fact of faith, how is that faith possible? How did the faith which is, come to be? How may we move from the subject to the object, move from talking about faith in one's experience to God as the source of all that is? This endeavour is carried on within the context of faith. The exposition of Scripture, of the classical creeds of the church, of the continuing witness of the church as she continues her expositions: all these are done within the context of faith and would not make sense, indeed would not be possible outside this context.

Our concern with faith is a religious concern. We are not here interested in rational abstraction about the meaning of faith. We are concerned with the theological exposition of its significance. We are at the centre when we say that the object of theology is faith in God. Hence, we must examine the implications of this twofold fact, the fact of faith and the fact of God as the source of faith. In this way, our discussions have religious significance. We become intellectualistic when we discuss religion apart from faith. And one does not have to be erudite and sophisticated to fall for this type of intellectualism. It can take place on all levels.

An example of this in the New Testament is what happened at Colosse. The theosophists at Colosse were interested in the Christian faith as grist for their particular 'philosophical' mill. 'Christianity provided a little more material for intellectual debate ....' Christ had become 'an appendage, one among others, to a theosophical construction.'[4] The whole heresy is summed up in the words of *Colossians* 2:8: 'See to it that no one makes a prey of you by philosophy and empty deceit, according to human tradition, according to the elemental spirits of the universe and not according to Christ.'

At Colosse, a fallacious philosophical construction excluded Christ as the revelation of God. At Galatia, an erroneous ethicoreligiocultic concern effectively nullified faith, and with it the activity of God in his free grace in Jesus Christ. That baneful and persistent kind of intellectualism which we call legalism was the outcome. Faith was replaced by a moralistic effort and Jesus Christ was replaced by the deeds that had to be done, cf. *Galatians* 3:15.

These two forms of the replacement of faith and of its object, God, the pseudo-philosophical and the moralistic, have been persistent ones in the history of the church. They are ever-present dangers.

A genuine and a pseudo-philosophy are not to be confused. There is the philosophising which assists the clarification of faith and its exposition. There is that philosophising that requires the repudiation of faith, whose assumptions would make faith mean-

---

4   Cf. F. C. Synge, *Philippians and Colossians*. London: S. C. M. Press, 1951, pp. 61, 62.

ingless or unnecessary. Each approach is to be evaluated upon its own merits. There must be no over-enthusiastic embracing, nor blank refusal a priori. Nor should there be the dogged persistence in maintaining a particular line of approach or method. This does not mean that examination of faith should not take place on other levels beside the theological. It is a productive exercise to deal with faith, for example as a psychological and as a sociological phenomenon. Nor are we to exclude philosophical approaches. Each may be contributory to our understanding. We shall not on principle reject secular approaches to these questions. We shall attempt to learn from them and be wiser. What we are here suggesting is one way of defining a theological treatment of faith.

III THE RIGHTEOUSNESS OF GOD

The Availability of God

God in his revealing activity has made himself available to man. Faith is the turning point from independence of God to dependence upon him. It carries with it the realisation that God did not will to remain independent of man. Man chose to defy him in rebellious disobedience, and chooses continuously so to do. That God has revealed himself and continues to reveal himself means that he will not remain independent of man's plight. The persistence of faith is the assurance for man that God has not so chosen, that he has not so withheld himself. In revealing himself to man God has joined himself to his creature with indissoluble ties. He has made man's destiny his concern.

All this is his choice in freedom. Shall man be granted the gift of believing unto life eternal? That this happens is because God has first chosen him, chosen that life eternal be possible for him, chosen that he himself be available for man. That God freely chose to relate in saving activity to the human is the presupposition of faith. God will not let man be independent from him, if man will have 'life', i.e. fulfillment, purpose, realisation. That God has willed to reveal himself to man, and that this revelation has been made, means that in dependence upon God, possible through the movement of God toward us, we fulfill the purpose of our creation.

Old Testament teaching

The God of the Old Testament is not far off, abstractly transcendent deity. God is indeed transcendent but, even though exalted far above the world, he turns to his creature seeking to create communion between man and himself. So we have an image of God walking in the garden, seeking communion with the newly formed creatures: cf. *Genesis* 3:8. There is the portrayal of the experience of Hosea and the harlot Gomer, serving as a symbol of Yahweh's relation to Israel. Hosea is to seek out and love the faithless woman in spite of her rejection of him and her waywardness. *Hosea* 1:2,3; 3:1. The whole of this book is a poignant portrayal of the prevenient mercy and love of God only to be renewed when beaten back by resistance and stubbornness. This is also expressed by the presentation of God as the living God, cf. *Deuteronomy* 5:26: 'Who is there that has heard the voice of the living God … as we have and has still lived?' Cf. *Psalm.* 42:2, 84:2, *Jeremiah* 10:10, 'But the Lord is the true God; he is the living God and the everlasting king.' So Elijah justifies his confrontation with Ahab with the simple words, 'Yahweh is living' *I Kings* 17:1. 'Just as life is a mysterious reality which can only be recognised, so God is a power which imposes itself on man and comes to meet him without his being always prepared for it.' For the Old Testament writer, the activity of God is not haphazard or promiscuous. It is directed specifically into certain channels. God makes himself known to his people. God's concern is with his people. The revealing of himself to Abraham — 'Then the Lord appeared to Abram and said, To your descendants I will give this land.' — is prospective of what he will do to create Israel, his people. God acts at the Exodus and creates the covenant with his people. It is through the covenant that the continuity of revelation is ensured. It is through the covenant concept that we find the unity of the revelation of God through the Old and New Testaments. The New Testament picks up the theme of the inscrutable, incomprehensible mercy and love of God

Justification by Grace Through Faith 15

in making himself known. It assumes and builds on what has been portrayed in the Old Testament. But more of that later.

That the initiative is with God is variously expressed in Scripture and in theology. 'We love because He first loved us' *I John* 4:19. 'Thou dost beset me behind and before and layest thy hand upon me' *Psalm* 139:5.

GRACE

The concept of prevenient grace lays stress upon the fact that whatever is done for the believer is done apart from any effort on his part. It is out of the insistence upon the fact that the initiative lies with God alone that the prevenience of grace is stressed. Wherever grace is to be found it is always prevenient. Indeed, if grace is not prevenient grace, it is not grace at all. The costly grace, which must be responded to with all our being, is no grace which we bestow upon ourselves. It is God who calls us to the supreme challenge, to accept the gift he gives to us out of his love and freedom. This is the gift of his free grace. Such grace preceded and precedes all our effort.

IV THE KNOWLEDGE OF GOD

God is made known in Jesus Christ

The God of Christian faith is God having made himself known in the person of Jesus Christ and continuing to make himself known in the Spirit in the church and, through the church, within the world. The object of Christian faith, the source of that faith, and the goal and end of that faith, its alpha and its omega, is God, the Father of our Lord Jesus Christ. For Christian faith the focal point is Jesus, confessed as Son of God, God with us.

That is it. God's revealing activity is focused in Jesus Christ. The Christian conviction is that God, the source of all reality has made himself decisively and ultimately known in Jesus Christ. The Christian takes with all seriousness that in fact, apart from what God has done in this revelation, he cannot be known at all decisively. For him, this is no abstract contemplation of a uniquely perfect manner of life, the supreme example of humanity, the paragon of innocence. Jesus Christ is God acting to achieve the purpose for which man was initially created. In this sense the act of creation is preliminary to that of revelation in Jesus Christ. Here God is revealing his righteousness, to use Paul's phrase. Or, as phrased elsewhere: 'God was in Christ reconciling the world to himself' *II Corinthians* 5:19. Here God dwells with man: 'And the word became flesh and dwelt among us' *John* 1:14. 'All this took place to fulfill what the Lord had spoken by the prophet: 'Behold a virgin shall conceive and bear a son, and his name shall be called Emmanuel which means God with us' *Matthew* 1:22,23.

The source of Christian faith is in the atoning act of God in Jesus Christ. Jesus Christ is the history of God with man and of man with God. '… in him it comes to pass that God is the reconciling God and man is reconciled man.'[5]

It is our experience of what God has done that makes possible our talking about what God is. It is the accomplished fact of reconciliation, experienced by one who has faith, that makes possible a presentation of God as merciful, gracious, longsuffering. Only as the revealing activity of God has been experienced may we speak of God in such terms. First God's saving act, then man's reconciliation with God, then witness to the fact, then discussion of the kind of God who has done it all, and of the nature of faith — that is the order of things. Who says faith says the revealing activity of God.

Revelation: the basis of theological discussion

It was this conviction that gave such burning importance to the early Christological discussions of the church. The fact that reconciliation had taken place in Jesus Christ, and that as a consequence man was placed in relation with God, was incontrovertible for the early church. The problem that this raised was so to define the person of Jesus, through whom this had been accomplished, that he was recognised as very God in activity. The New Testament recognised this, but did not give it theological elaboration. *Colossians* 2:9: 'For in him dwelleth all the fullness of the Godhead bodily.' 'The Word was with God and the Word was God' *John* 1:1-3. 'He who does not honour the Son does not honour the Father who sent Him' *John 5:23*, cf. *Hebrews* 1:2,3. This is no place to enter into a discussion of the intricacies of the Christological controversies. Suffice it to mention the Nicene formula which states, as the result of an energetic debate, that the son is *homoousios* (of one substance) with the Father.

---

5 K. Barth, *Church Dogmatics*. IV/1. Translated by G.W. Bromiley Edinburgh: T & T Clark, 1961, p. 158.

Justification by Grace Through Faith

Faith is of God

Faith is because God is. That is what has to be said first and foremost. God exists for faith to be. Do we seek for an evidence of the existence of God? We shall find it ultimately in the fact of faith. But God is not a static being. The God of the Christian faith is not the God of the philosopher. The God of Christian faith is the God who has moved towards man in condescension and in love. Without the initial movement of God towards man there would be no faith. God does not rest in impassive eminence, aloof in a deistic quietude, with no concern for man. God is the creator. God is Creator, that is to say, the being that God is a creative being. Implied in this, and portrayed in the Old and New Testaments is that God is active in the history of the creatures whom he has created. He is active to bring the creation to its proper end. God is. God is creative. God is active being. God acts to reveal himself to man, and in revealing himself to man reveals man to himself. God reveals himself. God is known as he reveals himself. Did not God reveal himself to man there would be no knowledge of this kind (so to speak) of God. Man would never penetrate the mysteries of the divine being. It is of God's freedom, and will, that is of his love, that he makes himself known to man. The first thing that has to be said concerning faith is that it is graced to man by this kind of God. Faith is of God. Christian faith is of a certain kind of God.

The righteousness of God: significance of the term

This activity of God moving toward man, revealing his love, in that he reveals himself; this revelation of the unwillingness of God that any should perish; this presence of God in human history directing the revealing events within a specific context of that human history; this extraordinary willingness of God to be present with man, accomplished in many different ways, and through many different means: this the Bible speaks of as the 'righteousness of God'.

In the Pauline vocabulary, as in the Old Testament, 'righteousness' refers primarily to an activity, not simply to a moral attribute. Thus it is far more than simply a juridical concept. We must thus beware lest in our employment of the terms; 'justice', 'righteousness', we chain the terms to the language and concepts of the law court with which we are familiar. Thus when Paul says that the 'righteousness of God is revealed', moving as he is within the context of Hebrew thought, he means that God is acting upon the plane of human experience, that God is doing something within the circle of human affairs. He is in this passage saying that God has effected the final demonstration of his saving activity. This has been done in the act of Jesus Christ, the act of incarnation. The argument of the early chapters of *Romans* leads up to the fulfillment of a necessity.

If man is to be saved, God must 'reveal his righteousness'. Such revealing of God's righteousness is of his free grace. So *Romans* 3:21,22. In saying that the revelation is 'apart from law' Paul is proposing that the revelation of God in Jesus Christ in no way has sprung up out of the legalistic atmosphere of Judaism. God's vindicating activity, that confers upon man a new status and makes a new state possible for man, has been graced to man. This has been done in Jesus Christ.

We have warned against an exclusively juridical interpretation of the term. This leads to the conception of God that requires strict justice, that asks fair measure for fair measure. For the Old Testament, the expression implies activity, relationship, fellowship, salvation. It is first and foremost a salvation word. 'God saves because he is just and He is just because He saves.'[6]

THE MEANING OF THE TERM 'RIGHTEOUS'

We should understand the term *tsadiq*, 'righteous', 'just' in its distinctive Old Testament sense according to the company it keeps. It is a salvation term, as for example in *Isaiah* 45:21: 'a just God and a Saviour'; *Zechariah* 9:9: 'just and having salvation'. God's justness lies in the fact that he saves his own. It is a word

---

[6] Ludwig Kohler, *Old Testament Theology*. Translated by A.S. Todd. Philadelphia: The Westminster Press, 1957, p. 34.

Justification by Grace Through Faith

indicating fellowship. 'God saves because he is just and he is just because he saves.' He is just who offers fellowship with himself and then intervenes to make that fellowship actual. This means also an activity and judgment since those who repudiate the relationship and oppose it become the object of God's righteous activity, now expressed in judgment.

Thus there are two types of activity to consider: saving the believer and afflicting the enemy: So Pharaoh acknowledges, 'I have sinned, the Lord is righteous' ('in the right' R.S.V.). *Exodus* 9:27. God wins victories, defeating the Egyptians and preserving the Israelites. He is deliverer. There is with this use of the word an overtone of triumph leading to prosperity. So the word can mean 'to cause to prosper'.[7] Every morning God shows forth his righteousness. He brings his judgment to light in his activity to save and, obversely, to judge (*Zephaniah* 3). So the praise of the Psalmist, 'The Lord is righteous; he has cut the cords of the wicked'. *Psalm* 129:4. God is *tsadiq* when he consumes the wicked but leaves a remnant in Israel, 'thou art just, for we are left a remnant that has escaped'.

The righteousness of God is related to his lordship. 'The Lord cannot exist without fellowship with those He rules.'[8] 'Justice' is not a juridical concept in Old Testament but is one of relationship.

The righteousness of God is an activity rather than a state. The word is a relationship word and implies fellowship. The Old Testament speaks of God's righteousness when he manifests his activity in history. For God is living. His righteousness is manifested in the appropriate manner in different situations. He commits no iniquity. He does not let sin go unpunished, nor let the good go unrecognised; He is merciful, for he will not let the sinner perish. He is God of love, following after the salvation of his people. He communicates his righteousness to his wayward people and justifies them. His righteousness is manifested. It is what God does that shows him as righteous. 'When it comes from God, righteousness

---

7   Cf. Norman Snaith. *The Distinctive Ideas of the Old Testament*. London: Epworth Press, 1983, pp. 8788.
8   Cf. Ludwig Köhler, *op. cit.*, p. 35.

is a transitive action and a visible manifestation of the being of Yahweh in his relations with man.'[9]

But this does not exclude the ethical significance of the term, as meaning 'that which conforms to a norm'. But for the Hebrew this norm is the character of God himself. We are dealing with a living person disposed in a certain way toward men, rather than an impersonal idea. Righteousness is not primarily a legal idea. It is such as it is seen in relation to God as judge. While the righteousness of God cannot be separated from the figure of God the judge, the predominant tendency is to the idea of salvation. The eighth century prophets use the term 'righteousness' in an ethical sense but the tendency is 'to shade off into a salvation sense'. In *Isaiah* the meaning of the term is chiefly soteriological. 'The word forms part of *SecondIsaiah*'s salvation vocabulary.[10]

God causes to prosper by acting to save. This is his righteousness. 'Judah will be saved and Israel will dwell safely and this is the name whereby he shall be called, the Lord our righteousness' *Jeremiah* 23:6. In such passages as *Isaiah* 45:2,3; 45:8; 51:5; 56:13; 59:16,17; 51:6 'righteousness' is equivalent to 'salvation', 'redemption'. Here the term 'righteousness' has come to mean 'salvation'. The righteousness of God shows itself in his saving activity. God saves the humble, those who trust in him, the humble of earth, for whom he has a special concern. 'Behold thy king cometh unto thee, righteous (*tsaddiq*, victorious) and saved', but also 'meek'. He rides on an ass, not on a war-horse. Here he proclaims his rule of peace.

DISTINCTION BETWEEN ETHICAL AND RELIGIOUS CONCEPTIONS OF RIGHTEOUSNESS

The 'ethical prophets' insisted upon right conduct. This insistence is based on their knowledge of God as the object of religion. For them ethics springs from a religious understanding. 'The standard by which they judged was not an ethical code. Their standard

---

9 Edmond Jacob, *Theology of the Old Testament*. Harper and Brothers,1958, p.95.
10 Cf. Norman Snaith, *op. cit.*, pp. 86, 87.

Justification by Grace Through Faith

was what they knew of the very nature of God himself. It was because they were so passionately religious that they were so insistently ethical. Knowledge of God came first, and the understanding of right action second.'[11]

THE PROPHETS' VIEW OF SIN.

The term can be used in two senses, as an ethical term, when it means transgressing a moral code, or as a religious term, when it means rebellion against God, and so being alien to him (*ibid.*) The religious man is ethical if and when his conception of God is ethical.

The prophets viewed sin as rebellion rather than as transgression.[12] God does not require sacrifices and substitutions but on the contrary (an adversative construction) he certainly does require mercy and kindness, e.g. *Micah* 6:7,8. The prophets were not Pelagian, not at all. They knew that human beings do not will to change their way of life. They cannot turn unless God turns them. 'The people is bent on turning away from me' states *Hosea* (11:7). Jeremiah utters the prayer, 'Bring me back that I may be restored, for thou art the LORD my God' (*Jeremiah* 31:18). Men do not repent and turn, but rather 'plunge headlong in their wickedness' (*Jeremiah* 8:4–7).

The poor in the land who were downtrodden were the particular objects of God's concern. So God will task special notice of their case. He will establish *tsedeq*, righteousness, in the land. God's will includes the establishment of justice in the land. 'Righteousness' stands for this will of God. So its reference to justice is incidental. It is on the way, here, to becoming a salvation word. 'It is incidental that *tsedeq* stands for justice. It is incidental because *tsedeq* actually stands for the establishment of God's will in the land, and secondarily for justice, because that in part is God's will.[13]

---

11   Ibid., p. 60.
12   Ibid., p. 65
13   Ibid., p. 70

Summary: there is a twofold significance of the word 'righteousness': (1) the standard, norm of judgment, which depends on the nature of God. (2) a persistent tendency to topple over into benevolence, and easily to have a special reference to those who stand in need of a helper.[14]

Paul

Paul moved within this realm of ideas when he used the expression 'the righteousness of God'. God has acted. The term points to a dynamic reality. So the Greek term *dikaiosune* (which in the Septuagint translates *tsedeq*) stands for this movement of God to deliver, and to vindicate, snatching his people from those who oppressed them — and emancipating them from their sins. So in the life, death and resurrection of Christ, God has been active to bring about the emancipation of man from sin by opening up the possibility of fellowship with himself. In Jesus, the righteousness of God creates relationship with man. God has done this. Man may find reconciliation then, not on the basis of fulfilment of prescribed moral duties, but by setting himself within the content of God's saving righteousness. God, in Jesus Christ has acted to put things right. The sinner is to have faith. Then he is 'justified' (the participle used in a cognate of *dikaio*).

C. H. Dodd provides an excellent summary of the meaning of the expression 'the righteousness of God is revealed' *Romans* 1:1617.[15] The term righteousness stands not only for a moral attribute, but also for an act or activity. So to say that God's 'righteousness' is revealed is to say that 'a divine act or activity is taking place manifestly within the field of human experience' (p. 38). In the Old Testament, 'righteousness' is derived from a verb whose primary meaning seems to be 'to be in the right' rather than 'to be righteous'. So 'to justify' means 'to put in the right', 'to vindicate', 'to give redress to'. Thus a judge or ruler is thought of as 'righteous' not so much because he observes and upholds an abstract standard

---
14 Ibid., p. 7.
15 Cf. *The Epistle of Paul to the Romans*. London: Collins, 1960.

Justification by Grace Through Faith

of justice, as because he vindicates the cause of the wronged'. (p. 38).

So in *Judges* 5:11, the phrase 'the righteous acts of the Lord' refers to the acts of vindication and deliverance which Jahweh has wrought for his people, in giving them victory over their enemies (p. 39). So the RSV translates, 'the triumphs of the Lord'. Cf. *Isaiah* 51:5 and *46:13* where the Moffatt translation renders 'victory' and 'triumph', respectively. But, Dodd points out, the word 'triumph' brings out only one side of the idea. 'For the. Hebrew word always carries with it the idea of the victory of right' (p. 39). The deliverance has for its end, not only the liberating of the people from their oppressors, but also from their sin. They are to be made 'righteous' in the sense of ethical quality. 'But always 'righteousness' is not primarily an attribute of God or of his people, but an activity whereby the right is asserted in the deliverance of man from the power of evil (p. 40).

In the prevailing thought of Judaism in the two or three centuries preceding Christ, it was assumed in the present age the cause of right was in eclipse. In the Age to Come God would act. He would bare his arm and establish good. Then his righteousness would be revealed.

Now Paul in these words of *Romans* 1:16,17 states, the righteousness of God 'is being revealed' (present tense), the present referring to the continuous activity of God. The revelation of God's righteousness is still in progress. 'It is real and even now in process.' The first part of *Romans* 1 presents the universal and dire need for the revelation of God's righteousness. Paul presents the world as under the dominance of sin, bringing terrible retribution in its train. Paul finds in the Gospel of Jesus Christ the answer of history to the aspirations of the prophets who looked for a decisive assertion and vindication of right against all evil in the world of men. The life and death of Jesus Christ, his resurrection, and the creation of the church through his Spirit constitutes a decisive act of God, an objective revelation of his righteousness.

V THE GRACE OF GOD

GRACE IS FREE

We have spoken of God's saving activity as the Biblical definition of the righteousness of God. In that God acts to save and to heal man, he is righteous. His activity is willed. God is free and in his freedom wills to act on behalf of sinful man. The initiative is thus with God who in face of man's plight moves toward him in love with the offer of salvation. This is God's grace. It is defined by what God has done. God is gracious. Grace is God's forgiving love towards man as sinful and gone astray. God is gracious: he is the kind of being from whom gracious acts spring. God's gracious activity has its source in his being: he is gracious.

To say that God is gracious is to lay stress upon human need. Grace is not grace unless it is free.[16] The ground of God's love manifested towards the sinner lies in his good pleasure, not in any qualities possessed by the person chosen by his grace. God's grace is completely gratuitous. It has its source in his good will, and is at no time dependent upon man's nature or deeds, not even when his nature is changed and good deeds are done. These are the result of grace, and are in no sense prerequisite to its origin or its continuance. God is never in man's debt. But man is always debtor to God.

---

16 Augustine, *Nature and Grace*, 4.

GRACE AS GIFT

Justification takes place freely through the grace of God. 'All are justified by his grace as a gift (*dorean*) *Romans* 3:24. This adverb *dorean* lays stress upon the character of God's grace as a gift. Grace gives. God's acting in righteousness is his gift to man. So the deed of grace is God's giving, the giving of Jesus Christ. 'He did not spare his own son but gave him up for us all' *Romans* 8:32. Here is God's gracious deed, the 'unspeakable gift' II *Corinthians* 9:15. In Paul's writing, the grace of God and the grace in Jesus Christ are equivalent, as his statement of *Romans* 5:15,17 indicates:

> 'For if many died through one man's trespass, much more have the grace of God and the free gift in the grace of that one man Jesus Christ abounded for many .... If because of one man's trespass, death reigned through that one man, much more will those who receive the abundance of grace and the free gift of righteousness reign in life through the one man Jesus Christ.'

In the New Testament emphasis is laid on the fact that since the grace of God is his gift, it is in no way dependent upon man's acts. It is in no way the result or outcome of man's deserts. We are saved 'not in virtue of our works ... but in virtue of ... the grace which he gave us in Jesus Christ. *II Timothy* 1:9. The coming of Jesus Christ was due entirely to grace. *II Corinthians* 8:9. The faith by means of which we were saved is itself the product of that initiating grace. 'By grace are ye saved through faith, and *that* not of yourselves: it is the gift of God' *Ephesians* 2:8. The term 'that' has reference is to the whole clause which precedes, since *touto* is a neuter singular. So we might render the sense as, 'the fact of having been thus saved is not of yourselves: it is God's gift'. 'As a result of free favour you are safe; but nevertheless you have been saved and therefore enjoy your present status.'[17]

In harmony with such statements where the term 'grace' is used, there are those which insist that when one turns to God it is

---
17 C.F.D. Moule.

because God has granted one, i.e. given one, that gift of repentance. Who says 'grace' says 'gift'. God gives repentance and forgiveness. It is said of Lydia from Thyatira that 'the Lord opened her heart to give heed' to what was said by Paul (*Acts* 5:31). That is very paradoxical. We believe and yet it is God who grants the gift of faith, without which we could not have faith at all. But one thing is certain. Faith is our own act. I myself must perform the act of faith. And yet it is equally certain that faith is not a creation out of our own resources.

God's grace is unmerited, unrestricted, free. Paul emphatically insists upon this, even if he does not come to theological clarity about his assertions. He leaves paradoxes to stand rather than to smooth over the problem by deemphasising the preeminence and the priority of grace. We shall examine these descriptions briefly. God's grace in unmerited. There is no resource that man possesses by means of which he has some antecedent claim upon God. No willing or doing of our own can put us in the debt of God, so that we may lay some claim upon his mercy, so that the word 'debt' becomes, at any point. an appropriate word. The believer is not one who works to earn his wages which then God duly pays him: Rather, God's grace is given freely, cf. *Ephesians* 2:8,9; *Romans* 4:4, 3:23. God's grace is universal, that is, it is open to all men. Thus, with the coming of Christianity barriers which once loomed very large are now broken down. Since all men are equally sinful in the sight of God, if any is to be saved it will be by an act of God's free grace in face of the impotence of all men. Thus whoever is saved will be saved in spite of whatever makes him count in the eyes of his fellow over against his fellow. There is nothing that makes a man count before God except the grace which God himself has freely given. So *Romans* 10:12–13: 'There is no distinction' 11:32; 'all … all' *Galatians* 3:28; 'neither Jew nor Greek etc.' *Romans* 2:11 'no respect of persons with God' *Colossians* 3:11; 'Here there cannot be Greek and Jew.'

The sovereignty of God's grace

Finally, there is another sense in which God's grace is presented. God is sovereign. Paul states this in the following manner, 'He hath mercy on whom he will, and whom he will he hardeneth.' *Romans* 9:18. What is being stressed here is that God's grace is not a sentimental benevolence that is at the beck and call of anyone and everyone. God is himself the arbiter of that grace, a grace which he disposes as he will. The emphasis is also made to give a divine basis for the observed fact that not all men are in fact willing to be recipients of God's bounty. There is no escaping God even in rejection. That is indeed one side of the sovereignty of grace. The other is that if a man is to be saved it is to be accounted the work of God. That not all men are saved and that this is empirically evident as well as theoretically possible is the other side of the coin. That God's mercy is offered freely is due to God's grace. That the few who accept are willing so to do is also due to God's grace. Should we temporalise this act of 'election' and introduce the notion of a determining decree we are in the hard realm of the predestination controversies. Be it said: it is better to argue about the grace of God than to ignore it.

Grace and faith

The righteousness of God, i.e. his righteous doings, his saving, activity is a manifestation of what God is. The source of man's hope and fulfillment, of his salvation, lies in the fact that God is grace. God is grace.

As we ask and answer the question, 'How shall we find a gracious God?', we confront two aspects of the doctrine. These we may call the objective and the subjective respectively. We approach the question objectively and subjectively. The question can be phrased in alternative forms. How can peace be concluded between a holy God and sinful man? By grace, but in a way which is adequately right. How can I lay hold of a gracious God? – in faith, itself the gift

Justification by Grace Through Faith

of God's grace. Talking about God's grace provides the 'objective' answer. Talking about man's faith provides the subjective.

These two answers correspond to the two ways of talking about faith. While faith is the experience of the believer, who has passed from death to life, it is grounded in the revealing activity of God. So both answers must be given. In the nature of the case, the question can only be answered from within the context of faith itself. Just as we can speak of faith only when faith is present, so we may speak only of grace as the source of that faith, when faith is presupposed. Are the two answers therefore distinct?

Grace is gratis. It reminds us that, do what we may, there is this point where we can do nothing, even when we have done everything. That is one. The other is that grace is of God and of God's freedom. The expression stresses again that if the product is of grace it is not of the nature of reward. If the product is really a gift it can by no means be earned. If God is the giver of a gift, then that God is gracious i.e. disposed to help man in his helplessness, and actually providing that assistance and rescuing man from his helplessness.

God's revealing of his righteousness is not of necessity, but of freedom. There is nothing inevitable about this gracious activity of God. It is by no means to be taken for granted. Our response to it must ever be one of surprise, praise, and glad gratitude. It is through grace that we are as believers all that we are. Grace is the source of all: the very faith by which we lay hold of the grace that saves is itself a gift of that grace.

Grace and faith are correlative terms. Grace is the source and faith is the instrument of God's righteousness. Faith is itself a product of that grace and that righteousness. Faith is thus 'graced' to us as God acts in righteousness. It is essential, theologically, to preserve the autonomy of God's grace. Only so can the Protestant assertion that man's hands are empty, and must always remain so when God's gifts are presented be preserved. Only so can the independence of God be preserved and the utter dependence of man, and in its turn the sinful depravity of man. To call into question, even in the slightest, the grace of God is to compromise his aseity, and unduly to exalt man to a place which because of his sin he can never occupy.

This is what happens in all forms of Pelagianism and of legalism. Here, in both cases, the basic presupposition is that there is that in man which is capable of creating relationship with God. There is that which God accepts. To some extent, the palms are not empty but contain something of worth. Sin is a problem that can be handled, at least to some extent, on the basis of one's own native resources. Such explanations lead to a modification, more or less radical, of the Christian concepts of sin, of grace, of judgment.

AUGUSTINE AND PELAGIUS ON GRACE

The classical exponent of grace was Augustine (born A.D. 396). Starting with the premise of man's depravity, and thus his utter inability to save himself, to do what his conscience told him he should do, in this reflecting the dilemma expressed in *Romans* 7, he insisted that since man's sin rendered him utterly incapable of good, if he were to find salvation it would be due solely to the grace of God. Since man is radically sinful the power of grace would have to be measured against the power of the indwelling. i.e. original, sin. Grace may even have to be irresistible. God is the source of grace, and because of man's condition, this grace must be given to him. Grace is gratis. Grace is of God. The first word that is to be said in relation to the removal of sin is that God is grace. Since the will of man is evil and can thus only pursue evil it can be set right only as God's grace enables it to be directed aright. The will is not free. In its unfreedom, i.e. in its bondage there is no way of escape. God's grace is the only answer.

It was in the discussion of these and implicated questions that Augustine came into heated conflict with Pelagius and his follower Coelestius. These taught that it was possible by the right direction of the will to avoid sinning. The implication of this was that, to quote an extreme statement of Coelestius, 'Our victory comes not from God's help but from our own free will.' Thus neither grace nor bondage were taken seriously. This is an ancient but persistent

Justification by Grace Through Faith

form of humanism and is to be found still in many forms of Protestantism. The constant threat is that the church confess in word, the Augustinian, the Pauline, stance but yet at heart, and in practice, be thoroughly imbued with the spirit of Pelagianism.

A concern similar to that of Augustine, to preserve the initiative of God and the incapacity of the human, led John Calvin to insist upon the priority of God's grace, and within this context to the doctrine of double predestination.

Such a concern has led Karl Barth to his radical insistence that there can be no knowledge of God apart from the grace of God as is manifest in Jesus Christ and to an interpretation of the Protestant insistence upon the aseity of God. In the light of this Christological centre. God is the centre of being and of knowledge (ontically and noetically), as he so often insists.

Augustine had presented the nub of the problem in his argument with the Pelagians as being that of what nature can be when assisted by Grace.[18] The possibility of sinlessness is not the issue, but how such sinlessness becomes possible. Augustine contends that it is by the grace of God only, rather than being an inherent capacity within human nature as Pelagius contended. All turns therefore upon the definition of grace. If sinlessness is impossible apart from grace, the crux of the matter lies in the way grace is defined. Grace is grace only as it is free.

So what is effected by the operation of grace upon man? Two important emphases emerge in Augustine which were to have incalculable influence in the centuries to follow. First, in his stress upon the depravity of man and the community of sinfulness in which man is bound. Man exists in a 'mass of perdition'.[19] He is bound up in the parcel of sinful humanity. 'Mass' is the unfortunate word. It leads to an evaluation of sin as some kind of quantity which has to be moved by what must almost appear as a quasi-physical substance. The substance of sin being removed by the opposite kind of substance, grace. This leads to the substantising of grace, i.e. the

---

18   Concerning Nature and Grace, 49.
19   Ibid, 5.

conceiving of grace in terms of a physical substance rather than in those of personal relationship. Second, the second emphasis in Augustine is aptly summarised by Mackintosh, 'through this grace, merits become attainable by which in accordance with the just rule of recompense, we can and ought to earn eternal life ... grace alone renders merit possible. Merit becomes possible when the supernatural grace of love has been breathed into the soul and since this love is God's bestowal, Augustine can say, in a famous phrase, that 'when God rewards our merits He but crowns His own gifts'.[20]

By these phases he continues the line of thinking which had emerged in the centuries that had preceded him.

THOMAS AQUINAS ON GRACE

The notion of merit had come to stay, and to form an integral part of the Roman Catholic doctrine. It is in Thomas Aquinas that we get the representative statement of Grace. He struggles to combine the ideas of grace and merit, ideas which seem contradictory to Protestants. His line of thinking is as follows: Man is in a state of corruption, following the Fall. While he has natural gifts, the supernatural gifts with which he was endowed at creation have been spoiled. In this state of corruption, fallen man needs grace in order to be the kind of person acceptable to God, in order that he may fulfill the requirements laid upon him by God. To produce meritorious works proportionate to eternal life man needs a more-than-natural force. He needs the force of grace. By the infusion of grace, there comes to be in man a *habit* i.e. a habitual tendency, which leads to good works, which God in his justice must recompense. Works done out of the infused 'habit' of grace i.e. the operation of divine grace which gives man's will a habitual tendency to love for God and man, are such that in justice God must recompense them.[21]

---

20 *The Christian Experience of Forgiveness*. London: Nisbet, 1927, p. 133.
21 Cf. Anton C. Pegis, *Introduction to Saint Thomas Aquinas*. New York: The Modern Library, 1948, pp. 655,659,660, 663, 664-6.

Justification by Grace Through Faith 35

Thomas taught that the source of grace is in God alone, 'it is impossible that any creature should cause grace'.[22] But in defining grace as substance, connecting it with merit and with the notion of infusion, and thus tying it to the sacramental and ecclesiastical machinery, he has quite distorted the New Testament teaching of grace, which is the free mercy of God. Merit is not a New Testament word.

It follows from Thomas' presentation of grace, that man cannot have the assurance of acceptance. In a section in which he deals with the problem, 'Whether man can know that he has grace?' Thomas considers that there are three ways of knowing something: by revelation. So Paul knew that he had grace because God revealed to him that his grace was sufficient (*II Corinthians* 12:9). But such a way to knowledge is exceptional. A second way is that a man may know something 'of himself'. But, since 'the principle of grace and its object is God, in this way no one can know that he has grace'.[23] What then is left? In Thomas's words, 'Things are known conjecturally by signs; and thus anyone may know he has grace when he is conscious of delighting in God and of despising worldly things, and inasmuch as a man is not conscious of any mortal sin ... Yet this knowledge is imperfect'.[24]

Summary of Thomas's teaching.

(1). Grace is of God.
(2). Man needs grace for eternal life.
(3). The infusion of grace makes him a certain kind of man
(4). As such, he performs meritorious deeds, acceptable to God.
(5). God rewards such deeds, and thus accepts the man whose habit of soul leads to their performance.
(6). Man may not be certain that he is accepted by God. His knowledge of acceptance is always imperfect.
(7). The offices of the church in the sacraments are the means of grace. Only as he is continually present at the mass and

---

22 Ibid., pp. 672673.
23 Ibid., p. 679.
24 Ibid., p. 680.

faithful in confession and penance can there be any hope of acceptance. What certainty he has depends upon the faithful performance of prescribed duties.

THE ANALOGY OF FAITH

We have already spoken of the prevenient grace of God. That is the theological way of stressing the consciousness that faith is no creation by man, on the basis of his inner resources, out of materials that are part and parcel of his makeup as a human being. Faith is not a natural resource, but is a gift. This has also been expressed by the phrase, 'the analogy of faith'. This expression has been employed in two different ways theologically: (1) as a principle of biblical interpretation: the Bible is to be interpreted by the analogy of saving faith in Christ. Thus a canon of judgment is provided for that which is more or less pertinent, more or less edifying, more or less at the centre of the message of the Bible. A principle of canonicity is provided.[25] (2) as a means of emphasising the dependence of faith upon the gracious acts of God's revelation. It is thus linked to the revealing word which is spoken by God. Had God not acted, spoken his word, faith would be impossible. Notice the clear statements of Calvin to this effect.

'Paul yokes faith to teaching as an inseparable companion (Calvin quotes *Ephesians* 4:20,21) .... There is a permanent relationship between faith and the Word. Take away the Word and no faith will then remain .... In understanding faith it is not merely a question of knowing that God exists, but also – and this especially – of knowing what is his will toward us ... we hold faith to be a knowledge of God's will toward us, perceived from his Word.'

Calvin then attempts to specify the content of this revealing Word that precedes and produces faith, for this Word is not merely a general knowledge of God's will for 'it is after we have learned that our salvation rests with God that we are attracted to seek Him ...

---

25 Cf. Alan Richardson, *Christian Apologetics*. London: S.C.M. Press, 1948, pp. 184188.

Justification by Grace Through Faith

the knowledge of God's goodness will not be held very important unless it makes us rely on that goodness .... It is then that Calvin is prepared to give his definition of faith:

> 'Now we shall possess a tight definition of faith if we call it a firm and certain knowledge of God's benevolence toward us, founded upon the truth of the freely given promise in Christ, both revealed to our minds and sealed upon our hearts through the Holy Spirit.'[26]

Thus, where there is no Word there is no faith. The divine and creative grace of God calls forth the response of faith. Thus 'the human act of faith is the analogue of the divine act of revelation.'[27] When God's Word is effective in man, the presence of faith is the outcome. The presence of faith is thus evidence of the accomplished work of God's revelation.[28]

PARABLES OF GRACE

In the teaching of Jesus it is sinners who are called upon to repent. *Matthew* 9:10-13. Jesus deliberately associated with the sinner and the guilty, and freely welcomed them to his salvation. Whereas the rabbis looked for the coming Messiah and the establishment of the kingdom when the law should be kept, Jesus deliberately associated with the sinful and called them to the kingdom. It was quite clear that attainment, merit, excellence of moral character were not prerequisite to the knowledge of God Jesus brought. He spoke of forgiveness and acceptance and offered them freely to all. There was a transvaluating of the idea of righteousness.

The problem of the Jewish righteousness was not that it was exclusive to the moralist. Jesus said it was not good enough. A select group of moralists was with great difficulty striving after the attainment of a righteousness. Jesus said this was not satisfactory. Setting himself over against the moralists of his generation he says, 'For I

---

26 Institutes, III. ii. 6-7.
27 C. Lovell Cocks, By Faith Alone. London: James Clark, 1943, p. 75.
28 For further elaboration cf. Karl Barth, Church Dogmatics I/1, translated by G.T. Thomson. Edinburgh: T & T Clark, pp. 260-283.

tell you, unless your righteousness exceeds that of the scribes and Pharisees, you will never enter the kingdom of heaven,' *Matthew* 5:20. The parable of the Pharisee and the Publican was expressly told in deliberate opposition to the teachings of the 'righteous' and to the attitude it engendered. It is prefaced by the words, 'He also told this parable to some who trusted in themselves that they were righteous and despised others ...' *Luke* 18:9.

The great problem with the state of these represented by the Pharisee was that the selfsatisfaction engendered as a consequence of the claim to righteousness led to an exclusiveness which became most emphatic in the rejection of Jesus. They placed themselves beyond hope and brought upon themselves their own rejection by Jesus, who turned to the unrighteous and offered them the 'more exceeding righteousness'.

In the parable of the Labourers in the Vineyard, the idea of merit is completely negated. A man is accepted not because of how much labour he had performed, but entirely out of the grace of the master, who gives to all as he will. The 'righteous' are represented by the objectors who have toiled through the day, the 'unrighteous' by those who come in at the end. On the basis of an agreement made in terms of quantitative remuneration, 'so much pay for so much labour', there can be no quarrel with the master, not even if he gives more to others who have worked less. An agreement is an agreement. On the basis of the agreement one cannot question the propriety of grace. So the comment, 'Take what belongs to you and go; I choose to give to this last as I give to you. Am I not allowed to do what I choose with what belongs to me? Or do you begrudge my generosity? So the last will be first and the first last' *Matthew* 20:14-16. 'To the seeking heart, He gives in grace all that the most obedient think they can justly claim.'[29]

---

29   H. R. Mackintosh. *op. cit.*, p. 109.

VI JESUS CHRIST: THE OBJECT OF FAITH

Personal disclosure

The Christian has faith in God. There is no other object of faith. To have faith in any other object is idolatry: to have faith in many objects is polytheism. The Christian is neither idolater nor polytheist. He has one object of faith and that object is God.

God is, for the Christian, object of faith before he is object of thought. For the Christian believer certain events are of decisive importance for faith. The Christian way of life is not first and foremost a way of thought. It is, rather, a way of life. The early Christians called it 'The Way'. They had come to have faith because of certain events that had recently happened among them. Those events have never been forgotten by the church. They never could. For what happened in the first century is all-important for faith. What happened was that God came among men in the person of Jesus who was believed on as Lord. The church has always remembered that when it has been faithful to its Lord and when it has maintained its faith.

What happened then was not that another teacher came and announced eternal truths of reason, and called for adherence to a school of thinking. What was called for was no mere intellectual response to a different philosophy from what had been known up to that time. In Jesus, God made demands upon man, demands which called for total commitment, unconditional discipleship. He called for 'followers', not simply pupils. Response to him was not appropriate if it became only a mode of thought. Response to him was to be a total reorientation of a way of life. Jesus' announcement was not an abstract statement about the absolute. It was the concrete call, 'Repent! The Kingdom of God is among you!'

Something happened. Jesus came among men, announcing the good news of God's love, but also making that love possible. He was the embodiment of God's love in the form of a human being. 'God with us' — that was the event. 'God was in Christ' that is the resting place for Christian faith. 'The Word became flesh' — that is the unique revelation of God known to Christian faith. Jesus Christ is the unique object of faith. Jesus is the Christ. Jesus is Lord — that is the unique confession of the Christian believer, who could never prove it but who testifies to its truth. One does not argue another into that faith. One offers an invitation.

So, when we ask, 'What is the meaning of Christianity? What is a Christian?' we would be at the very centre of things if we answered: 'A Christian is one who in his total life acknowledges Jesus as God. He is one who has faith. He is one whose object of faith is Jesus.'

Jesus is so described in certain familiar passages in the New Testament. We are admonished to look unto Jesus 'the author and finisher of our faith' (*Hebrews* 12:2) and, at the close of the Scriptural canon, he is similarly described, 'I am Alpha and Omega, the beginning and the end, the first and the last' (*Revelation* 22:13). He, as the object of faith, invited men to have faith in him, for to have faith in him was to have faith in God. 'Let not your hearts be troubled; believe in God. believe also in me' (*John* 14:1). He called for faith in himself, and faith in him was identical with faith in God, since he and the Father are one (*John* 10:30).

But what do we mean when we speak of Jesus as the object of faith? To enable us to understand more clearly we shall ask for a moment that you think of something, anything. Let us say that you thought of a ship. Now, while the idea 'ship' was in your mind you had a specific object of thought. 'Ship' was the object of your thought. You are thinking now of something in some way known to you, within range of your experience. Your thinking has to do with something that you have known. To be able to have an object of thought means that you hold before your mind something that is in some way available to you. Now let me ask you to think of a person, someone, anyone. Let us say that you thought of two persons: one whom you have never met, say, Winston Churchill, and another you know with some degree of familiarity. You have two objects of thought: you have read of Churchill in the newspapers, and have an acquaintance with the facts of his life and his career and character. But you do not know him as you know the friend about whom you also thought. Both were objects of thought, but with the friend there is a very important difference. The difference is that you came to know him differently. You have read about Churchill, but you have had personal contact, conversations with the friend. That makes all the difference. So you may hold that friend not simply as an object of thought, but also as an object of trust. You would entrust your goods and your life to him.

Disclosure and response

You can come to know another person only as there is a personal disclosure to you. If the other person does not disclose himself, if he does not will to let himself be known, if he withholds himself from you, he will never become an object of trust. He may well be an object of thought, but never an object of trust. Before there is personal trust there is personal disclosure. There is the willingness to make oneself available to the other. Only so can there be genuine personal relationships. Only so can one know another in a relation of personal trust. Of course, we trust other people, some of whom we know very little, with all sorts of things. It should be clear that it is personal trust we are speaking of here.

But there is something else that must be added to this. The one who discloses himself or is willing to disclose himself must be acknowledged, received. There must be personal receptivity on the part of the other to whom the disclosure is to be made. I may be very willing to open myself in friendship to another, but unless there is receptivity and response upon their part there will be no relationship of mutual trust between us. The object of faith must disclose himself and must be received, that is to say, must be accepted as trustworthy.

If God is to be trusted he must make himself known. He must disclose himself to man. Man cannot by searching find out God (*Job* 11:7). If God does not take the first step toward man he will forever remain unknown. God takes this first step. God makes himself known. God comes to man. God becomes man. In infinite love and condescension, he takes our mortality and dwells among us in the tent of our flesh, 'being made like unto his brethren' (cf. *Hebrews* 2:17). God takes the initiative and comes to men. In that coming to men the great invitation is made. God is willing to open himself to men: in fact in Jesus Christ it has been done. It has become event. Have faith in God! Trust him! Make him now the object of faith, who has shown himself to be willing to be such! God came into human history and calls men to trust him and shape their personal histories by that faith-knowledge.

It should be clear that God's demand for faith is not simply the call to add a little bit more to the fund of our information. Listen to this statement, 'My father retired in the country.' I am sure you understand the words. In fact, you know something which you did not know before you read these words. Your fund of information has now perceptibly increased. You are just a little more knowledgeable. Or take another statement, 'My car is in good working order.' Once again, you know a little bit more than you did before. On the basis of these two bits of knowledge, you can draw conclusions and implications which you were not able to draw before. You have something more to think about should you so desire.

But supposing I were to say, 'Jesus Christ is the Son of God.' What then? In what way may I understand this statement? At once it is obvious that it is not just another piece of information that I can tuck away in the recesses of my mind. For I can only come to know what it means as I come to know God, and this can never be simply by learning another fact I did not know before. For there is all the difference in the world between believing a fact about somebody and trusting someone with all your heart.

The fact which you have believed may turn out to be true: there is such a thing as gossip and slander! But it is through trust that personhood comes into being. I may believe certain facts about Jesus, but to believe facts about Jesus is, by no means, the same as to trust him. To think about, to learn about, Jesus is not identical to trust in him. In fact, the only guarantee that our thinking about, our knowing about, Jesus will be at all adequate is that we have already come to have faith in him. Faith must always precede correct understanding of him. Religion always precedes theology.

God comes to man in Jesus and offers himself as the object of man's trust. But man cannot create faith. Man is sinner and cannot help himself. The God that judges man in his sinfulness offers him the gift of life: as he does. He calls for faith. We have seen that this call to faith is not the call to add another piece of information to man's already existing knowledge, as if he could easily acknowledge, 'Ah yes! Jesus is God's son. How interesting! I am very grateful to you for the information' and then pass on to other things. Faith is not merely persuading oneself to accept propositions or creeds and, in that way, adding to the fund of one's information. Faith is radical trust, the commitment of all that one has to the God who is manifest in Jesus Christ. Faith is unconditional discipleship. Faith is not 'seeing the argument'. It is not 'believing' that a piece of information is true. Faith means accepting God in Christ as the ultimate reality by which my life shall be guided, as the origin and goal of my life. Faith means that Jesus becomes the Alpha and Omega of my life, that my life becomes life of personal trust in him.

Faith of this kind means worship. Worship is the whole-souled devotion of the trusting to what is the source and end of his being, as he is acknowledged to be such. Faith means worship. Jesus becomes the object of worship. Christians worship Jesus Christ. Even the Romans knew this. A very early letter of one Roman official to another speaks of Christians assembling and singing a hymn to

Jesus as to God. Faith means worship and as Jesus is the object of faith, so he is the object of worship.

We may truly worship only God. To worship any less is to become an idolater. It was the realisation of this truth that drove the church to strenuous opposition to Arianism, which denied the reality of the oneness of Jesus with God thus making him other than God. This cannot be. We know that this cannot be when we have trusted Jesus as God. If Jesus is not very God and I believe and worship him as such, I become an idolater and my devotion is misplaced. But Jesus is also very man. For if he be not true man, he has not reconciled man to God: he has not reconciled me to God. My faith would be similarly misplaced. 'God was in Christ' (II *Corinthians* 5:19). 'The Word was made flesh and dwelt among us' (*John* 1:14). Jesus Christ, the object of faith, is true man in whom sin is both judged and overcome. Sin is judged by God and overcome by man. 'Behold the man!' Jesus Christ, the object of faith, is very God for, were he not, we would be 'yet in our sins'. It is on the basis of our reconciliation that we confess: 'God was in Christ'.

We can worship that which is the object of faith. We can reduce neither the Godhood nor manhood to talk about faith, or to thought about faith. Jesus Christ is the object of faith, for the only proper object of faith is God himself.

We are now ready to make a summary statement in answer to the question, 'Who is the object of our faith? The object of our faith is the living God, made known in Jesus Christ, through a cross, loved as a Saviour and obeyed as a Lord.

To say that Jesus is the object of faith is to say that God has made himself known in revealing activity. God lives for faith to be. The living active God becomes man. God did something. God made himself known. He did not send someone other than himself to impart information about himself that could simply be learned. He came himself, and in the revelation demanded personal trust. He did simply propose a set of new directions to the human creatures from a lofty height, then to be heard no more. He became man. Jesus is God's speech. He is the 'Word of God'. The Son is God speaking, and this speaking is the giving of himself. He became man. He assumed manhood into himself. He went to the Cross.

That all was the revelation of God. Something new *happened.* What was unknown became known. The mystery hidden from generations was manifest (*Colossians* 1:26). It was God who manifested himself. The Good News is of what God did. He willed to disclose himself, so that now he could be fully known. He moved toward the human in personal self-disclosure, as we have said earlier. The mystery (and the Greek term in the New Testament means 'that which was hitherto unknown') now became known. God willed to love man. God willed to save man. God willed that his love be known by man.

Between man's sin and God's salvation there stands a Cross. That did not just happen as an accident of history. The Cross reveals God. What is God like? To answer this question we must look to the Cross where we shall see the judgment of God against man, *the* man, and through that judgment the love of God for all men. We should not ask, 'What is God like?' For the Cross does not tell us what God is like. Rather it shows us God in action. God is not like Jesus. God was in Christ. In the activity of Jesus we see the activity of God.

It is in faith that the cross of Jesus is seen as the revelation of God. The God who was once made known in the Incarnation and in the Cross continues to be known and loved. It is as the cross is preached that God comes to be known and continues to be known. As witness is borne to the reconciling activity of God, there continues to take place the miracle of renewal as the presence of the same God who was present in Jesus becomes a reality in the life of the believer.

Proclamation, *kerygma*

The message of Christianity is announcement. It is proclamation. The declaration is made that God is with men, and that God is for men. The message of Christianity is also invitation and demand. It says because God has acted to redeem, response is to be made, a decision must be made, a judgment (the Greek word is *krisis*) is necessary. In face of the activity of God, man must make up his mind. Man's will must be directed toward or against the will of God there expressed. The invitation is an invitation to faith, which is at the same time an invitation to gratitude. What is demanded is the outflowing of gratitude to God for the faith that is given with the gratitude, because both are response to the demand of the sovereign God. Love calls for responsive love. In face of the sin that so dominates man, God's love in Jesus Christ invites to responsive love and gratitude.

It is then that God is known. God is not known unless he is known as Lord. The demand made is for nothing less than all. This is the risk of faith, that we shall lose all as we follow the demand. But, since it is God who calls us, we are not left with an alternative choice. There is no alternative to the alternative. We let our life be dominated by a new love or we do not. We either become different kinds of slaves or we do not. There is no middle way in which we can make a partial response, or escape by failing to respond.

Thus we make connection with the introductory remarks. Man cannot create faith. Faith is not the learning of some new facts about history, about another character. The other person cannot be known unless he discloses himself, makes himself available. That is what God has done in Jesus Christ. But unless the disclosure finds response, knowledge is only potential. As personal response is made to personal disclosure the knowledge of persons takes place. Only so can there be personal knowledge at all. Such is the knowledge of the believer. In such a manner God in Christ, by becoming the object of faith, becomes known to the believer. This is what the New Testament means by 'knowledge' and by 'revelation'. This is clear in the following words, contained in the beautiful prayer in *Ephesians*, ' I pray that the God of our Lord Jesus Christ, the all-glorious Father, may give you the spiritual powers of wisdom and vision, by which comes the knowledge of him' (1:17 NEB).

Justification by Grace Through Faith

Such revelation and such knowledge is not merely the knowledge of assent. It is the knowledge of faith. It is not the knowledge of the pupil, but the knowledge of the disciple. Its source is in God. Its object is the activity in Jesus (verses 19–20). Its context is the church (verse 23).

This being the case, we can never come to faith in Jesus Christ by means of a process of proof. We are not 'proved' into being Christians. By the same token, we cannot be proved out of being Christians. We cannot prove the necessity of faith. There is all the difference between being convinced that a theorem is true, that a scientific explanation is highly probable, or that a philosophical argument is valid and knowing another person. Faith is of the order of the latter, of the order of personal truth.

If we cannot prove our faith, we can witness to it. We can tell the story of the one who is its object, and his coming to us in love. That is what the New Testament writers do. Of course there is argument and explanation. There always is. But the argument and the explanation is always employed in the service of some aim or other. The New Testament believers testify. They bear witness to what happened to them. Whatever lines of argument they employ, they employ in the service of this witness, and in the context of the community of witness (which sometimes has serious problems). They do not say, 'We shall prove to you by the following reasons, a, b, c, d ..., that it could not have been otherwise than it was.' Or, 'You must give rational consent on the basis of our reasoning, and then call that 'faith'. That was reserved for a later rationalism. They speak quite differently. God moved toward them. He disclosed himself to them. What they came to know was of the nature of revelation, not discovery. So they asked for the same response that had been demanded of them, for the willing response. They witnessed. Their language is the language of testimony. The English word 'martyr' is a transliteration of the Greek word which means 'witness'. The English term has come to mean one who witnesses in death for his conviction and for his faith. But in the New Testament all Christians were *martures*, witnesses. The word is very often used by Paul to characterise his work (cf. *Acts* 18:5,20,24; 23:11). It is used of the earliest apostolic preachers to characterise their work (*Acts* 8:25). The following passage clearly sets forth how faith and how Jesus Christ as its object are commended to the believer:

> 'That which was from the beginning, which we have heard, which we have seen with our eyes, which we have looked upon, and our hands have handled of the word of life; (For the life was manifested, and we have seen it, and *bear witness*, and show unto you that eternal life, which was with the Father and was manifested unto us;) That declare we unto you, that ye also may have fellowship with us and truly our fellowship is with the Father, and with his Son Jesus Christ.' *I John* 1:1–3.

Faith and Jesus Christ as its object are commended by witness. As witness is borne, God himself draws near with the disclosure of his personal presence, and that presence is the demand for faith, for unconditional trust. This is the way the good news is preached. This is the way God in Christ becomes known.

God known only to faith

The very existence of faith rests upon the accomplished fact of Jesus Christ as the revelation of God. The accomplished redemption in Jesus Christ is apprehended through the faith that redemption makes possible. At all points, and especially here, we stress again the priority of God's act. Faith is not an act created out of his own resources by the religious subject. It is not a possibility inherent in human nature as such, that is in the 'natural man'. We have already discussed the meaning of grace. Faith is the gift of grace. It is not an inherent quality of graceless man. It rests upon and comes into creation through the act of Jesus Christ as that act is kept alive in the community of believers, the church. Faith is thus bound to Christ, inevitably springing from him. Were this not so, anthropology would replace theology. Because this is so, Christian theology must consist in Christology.

Jesus Christ is the centre of Christian theology because Jesus Christ is the source of faith, and faith is the subject matter of theology. There is a referent for faith. Who says faith says God. When the Christian says faith, he says God in Jesus Christ. 'For it is the God who said, "Let light shine out of darkness" who has shone in our hearts to give the light of the knowledge of the glory of God in the face of Christ.' *II Corinthians.* 4:6. 'God was in Christ'. 'God with us' — these are the themes which lie at the basis of Christian faith.

But what is meant by these two assertions: first, that God is revealed in Jesus Christ, and secondly, that faith is dependent upon this prior act? It is as we approach the answer to the first of these questions that we see that an understanding discussion of the basic facts of Christianity cannot be one that is made in theoretical detachment. Who can talk of sin, of judgment, of renewed life, in detachment from the reality to which these terms point? At all points our theology should keep in touch with our religion. Here especially.

God is known in Jesus Christ. Between this and the abstruse theological and seemingly hairsplitting dogmatisms of the various Christological creeds there seems to be all the difference in the world. But the definitions attempt to preserve the reality of the divine in the presence of Jesus Christ. That is what must be preserved if the Christian religion is true. And who is the God that is revealed in Jesus Christ, who is this God of faith, of Christian faith? What is the nature of the reality which is presented to us at this point. What is the essence of God, this substance with which the Son is *homoousios* (*of one substance*)? What is the nature of this God who was 'in Christ'? The answer is that the God revealed in Jesus Christ is the God who will not be content with man, as man has made himself to be, but who will do everything that may be done to relieve man of his distress, and bring him back to life and love and beauty. The Bible speaks of finding the lost, of the royal welcome for the living dead (*Luke* 15:11-24). It is the portrayal of what God has done already. He is the Father who has given all and now waits. He gave himself in Jesus Christ.

We speak of what God is, on the basis of what God has done. We can only confess it. We can never prove it. Thus the assertions of the apostles' creed are: 'I believe in God the Father ... etc'. The only religious significance of God is of a God who is believed in. The God revealed in Jesus Christ is the God who is known only to faith. The corollary of revelation is faith. The corollary of the revelation of God in Jesus Christ is faith in Jesus Christ, i.e. Christian faith. It is only in faith that God is known. It is only on the basis of this faith that God can be spoken of at all. 'We speak that which we do know.'

What Scripture teaches about the knowledge of God

It was under the influence of the rationalism characteristic of the Greek mind that the term 'knowledge' came to be employed of an intellectual content that could be abstracted from experience. In fact, the terms 'abstraction' and 'knowledge' may be identical for the idealistic tradition which had great influence over the history of Christian theology. But the world of the Bible is a very concrete world. It delights in concrete imagery, such delight often being blunted to us, because of a passive familiarity with it. Within the context of the Judaeo-Christian tradition 'knowledge' was of the most concrete kind possible, and the verb 'to know' was so far removed from the abstractions of philosophical idealism that it could stand for the act of sexual intercourse between man and wife, not simply as a physical act, but as the focal point of personal relations of love and tenderness that were productive of life. So Th. C. Vriezen entitles his sixth chapter (in *An Outline of Old Testament Theology*),[30] 'The Nature of the Knowledge of God in the Old Testament as an intimate Relationship between the holy God and Man.' He thereafter points out that

> "the knowledge of God is something altogether different from having a conception of God, by which one defines the

---

30 Massachusetts: Charles and T. Bramford, 1960, pp. 128-147

nature of God. It is not ontological but existential: it is life in the true relationship to God.'[31]

The analogy of such knowledge of God is not to be found in modern scientific method, not the classificatory knowledge of objects. Rather, it is to be found in the knowledge of relationship, of communion that knowledge of being in relation with a person that makes special demands, moral demands. Such knowledge of God is to be found as God has made himself known. This he has done in his acts in history. Not promiscuously, but in the history of that people whom he has chosen. The covenant he made with Israel is the locus of the knowledge of God. Communion with God is to be found within the covenant relationship. Knowledge of God is directly related to obedience of God's will. Men know God by the hearing of his Word, the word 'hear' also meaning 'to obey'. 'For I desire steadfast love and not sacrifice, the knowledge of God rather than burnt offerings.' *Hosea* 6:6. The activity of God is the norm for the activity of men who 'know' him. Out of the intimate relationship between God and men, there springs righteousness in man that is akin to that of God, cf. *Jeremiah* 9:24 'Let him who glories glory in this, that he understands and knows me, that I am the LORD who practice steadfast love, justice and righteousness in the earth; for in these things I delight, says the LORD'; *Amos* 3:2 'You only have I known of all the families of the earth; therefore I will punish you for all your iniquities.' That God knows man may mean that correction is necessary. The element of judgment is also a covenant theme.

The same understanding is continued in the New Testament. A key passage is that of *Matthew* 11:27:

> 'All things have been delivered to me by my Father, and no one knows the Son except the Father and no one knows the Father except the Son and any one to whom the Son chooses to reveal him.'

---

31 Ibid., p. 129.

The Son is the one in unique relation to God, the one through whom the knowledge of God is brought to the world. If Jesus does not reveal God there is no true knowledge of God in the world. So the Fourth Gospel stresses the personal and moral dimensions of the knowledge of God.

But we have asserted that the faith by which the revelation of God in Jesus Christ is known is itself the gift of God. Or, to put it in other terms, the revealing of God in Jesus Christ is a present reality to one who has faith. If God is not present here and now there is no knowledge of God. This is the basis of the Christina doctrine of the trinity, which is not fundamentally a purely intellectual problem. But we cannot go into that here.[32]

JUDGMENT AND SALVATION

The God who is known to us in Jesus Christ is the God who judges us, who condemns us utterly, whose judgment upon us is a destructive judgment, from which there is no appeal.

Thus in so judging us the radically destructive nature of sin is revealed, and the predicament of the human. In such a revelation of himself, God reveals what man is. Only as God is revealed can man himself be known. Man knows himself, if at all, only as God makes himself known. The human reality is known only as the divine reality is revealed. How may we speak of love and mercy and welcome, and fatherhood in reference to such judgment on such a creature man? How can we who are such men find ourselves welcomed into our father's house, with the fatted calf made ready amid the laughter and song of welcome. Surely, we belong outside! Surely this is not for us! It cannot be that we have returned! The unmanageable and inexplicable thing is that we did. We, the sheep who belonged on the hills, had wandered off and became lost. But we are found and carried aloft and again there is song and welcome and great joy. It can never be. But it has been and it is! Our part is now to join in the rejoicing (*Luke 15*).

---

32 For further discussion, see Edward W. H. Vick, *Speaking Well of God*. Nashville: Southern Publishing Association, 1979.

It did not just happen. It was willed. Between man and God there stood and stands the fact, the continuing fact of sin. Between God and man there stands a life of incarnation and a Cross. Before the festal shouts and songs of joy there is the fight and the victory. That means the cross. And that was what God willed. God was in Christ. It is God who appears, who goes to the cross, who is victor over death. The initiative is pressed to the destruction of sin, and of man who is sin. But before it all and through it all there is the will of God. It was the will of God to suffer for the creature, such suffering as is beyond human measure.

> 'But none of the ransomed ever knew
> How deep were the waters crossed,
> Nor how dark was the night that the Lord passed through
> Ere He found his sheep that was lost.'

Jesus Christ is the concretion of God's will. That God himself has become man in the redemptive event, Jesus Christ, indicates that it was always his will so to become. In time we see the expression of the will of God in Jesus Christ. So Jesus Christ is the external manifestation of that which was hidden in the secret of God's being before the incarnation. He is the revelation of the mystery, 'the mystery hidden for ages and generations but now made manifest to his saints' *Colossians* 1:26. Jesus Christ is the ultimate speech of God.

In the Fourth Gospel he who was made manifest in the flesh is called the Word, the logos, and is identified with God. We here make contact with observations made previously. It is through the Word that faith is created. To say contact with the Word is to say revelation of God. God reveals himself. His word is made manifest. That Word is Jesus Christ. And whenever God has made himself known, and now continues to make himself known, *dikaiosune*, it is the Word, Jesus Christ that is known.

VII FAITH

Faith and the Spirit

The Spirit is the Spirit of Jesus Christ. To put on Christ was to be endowed with the Spirit. No sharp distinction is drawn in the New Testament between the Risen Christ and the Spirit. To believe, to acknowledge the Lordship of Jesus, to confess him as Christ and to be possessed of the Spirit are synonymous in the New Testament. So Paul can ask as a matter of course, 'Did you not receive the Spirit when you believed?' *Acts* 19:2. All Christians were considered to possess the Spirit. There was no exclusive prerogative for the few, for the 'spiritual' in the church. Rather the life of faith is a life in the Spirit, walking by the Spirit, being led by the Spirit, living by the Spirit. The Spirit guides into all truth. The Spirit makes God known, and to know in the biblical sense, is to be in personal relationship, cf. *Galatians* 5:16,18,25; *Romans* 8:4,14.

Thus, to assert that faith is a product of a fruitful contact with the Word of God is not to assert that a certain body of knowledge has now become available to us that was not available before in the sense, as Kierkegaard calls it, of 'paragraph material'. One has the feeling that objections to a doctrine of revelation that applies it to the believer in the here and now of faith experience have missed the point that what is being spoken of is life in genuine and fulfilling relationship, not an increment in an intellectualistic knowledge, which may be held in theoretical detachment from religion.

Revelation in Jesus Christ is not the purveying of a set of facts about an historical figure. It is the entering into genuine relationship with him. For this, the closest analogy is that of genuine relations with another human person. Faith is not a static, closed phenomenon. It has its being in lived human history. ' ... Faith is movement and happening, it is life, fulfilled life .... Faith today, as always, appears as an event ... Faith is not some kind of innate truth of reason ... Nor is it a purely inward happening ... Rather faith comes into being as the consequence of the witness of faith. And it depends for its nourishment on the constantly renewed witness, the Word of faith.'[33] If witness to faith is effective, the presence of God in Christ is made manifest through it. At any rate, there is no creation of faith without the intervention of the Word. Faith feeds on the Word of God, upon the word of witness. Without it faith could not be. And the Word is Jesus Christ.

This then is the real religious basis of the *analogia fidei* as an hermeneutical principle. For, it was asserted, certain parts of Scripture have a closer touch with this witness to Jesus Christ, and the revelation of God in him, that leads to the creation of faith. So for Luther, and for many another, there is virtually a canon within the canon of scripture. The criterion is that of witness, clarity of witness, to Jesus Christ on the part of the writer, as well as testimony to the centrality of faith.

The point at issue is that of the authority of Scripture. What principle shall govern what in Scripture we shall take as important? What shall we take as the most important? It is a matter of use, that is to say of reading. Those parts of Scripture which are the most widely read and considered will be most influential in the thinking and practice of the church. Why is it that some portions of Scripture assume in this practical way a greater importance than others? That is the question. The principle of the analogy of faith states that it is because of the clarity of their witness of Jesus Christ and to faith in him. Luther could, in applying this principle, be very emphatic in this rejection of certain portions of Scripture. For example, he called the epistle of *James* 'an epistle of straw' because he did not find in it a clear statement of justification by faith in Jesus Christ.

---

[33] Gerhard Ebeling, *The Nature of Faith*. Translated by Ronald Gregor Smith. Philadelphia: Fortress Press, 1961, pp. 21, 24, 25.

We only have to consider which passages of Scripture are read frequently and which passages are read only infrequently or not at all in the worship and devotion of the church to see that selection takes place. The next step in understanding this is to ask what the reason for such selection is, and what it implies.

A PRELIMINARY DENIAL

Faith, *fiducia*, is not belief that something is the case. Faith is not the acceptance on authority (that something is so). Faith is not confidence (in a thing). All of these are involved in faith. None is identical with it.

The word 'faith' is not a synonym for 'belief'. It is true that we often use these words interchangeably. People often mean the same when they use the term 'Christian belief', as when they use the term 'Christian faith'. Now notice something interesting. In English we do not have a verb 'to faith'. So the verb 'I believe' must do double service since we do not have, in English, two verbs: 'to believe', 'to faith', corresponding to the nouns 'belief' and 'faith'. So, we have to take care here. Otherwise confusion is inevitable.

The following examples illustrate that there are at least three meanings the expression 'I believe' may have. (1) I believe that it will be fair weather tomorrow. (2) Since the newspaper said so, I believe the story. (3) I believe in penicillin. The respective meanings are quite clear. In case (1) 'I believe' means, 'I have some grounds for holding, but I do not know for certain, that it will be fair weather tomorrow.' In case (2) 'I believe' means, 'I accept as true on authority', while (3) means 'I have confidence which will lead me to act in one way rather than in another.' Under certain circumstances, I shall take rather than refuse penicillin.

WHAT FAITH IS NOT

To conduce to clarity of definition, it is often wise to make some explicit denials. In our case, we shall indicate what faith is not, so that before we engage in a description of its Christian sense, we may anticipate and avoid certain misunderstandings from the outset.

(1). Faith is not belief as intellectual assent. This has been called the intellectualist distortion of faith. *Fiducia* is not *assensus*. *Fiducia* is not a creation of the intellect.
(2). Faith is not a creation of the will, the result of the socalled 'will to believe'. This has been called the 'voluntaristic distortion of faith'.
(3). Faith is not another work, the one which God will accept.
(4). Faith is not a mystical awareness, a praeterrational experience, issuing from the 'natural man'.
(5). Faith is not a turning of man to God.
(6). Faith is not a state of being, a *habitus,* a quality of the inner self which enables man to act aright.
(7). Faith is not intellectual assent, for example: the acceptance of an historical truth on the basis of sufficient evidence.

By observing linguistic usage in order we can indicate the ambiguities connected with the use of the terms 'faith' and 'belief' and thereby clarify legitimate theological usage of the term 'faith'. To this end, look at the following expressions: 'I believe I have met you before.' 'I believe what you say.' 'I believe in penicillin.' 'I believe in you, my son.' In each of these cases the expression 'I believe' has a different significance. In the first case, it expresses confusion, with a slight leaning towards recognition. It means 'I think but I am not sure.' In the second case, 'I believe' means, 'I accept as true', or 'I give consent.' 'I assent.' The content of what was said would have to be further examined to define further the meaning of the verb. In the third example, the term means 'I have confidence in something'. The final example goes beyond this. There the term means, 'I have confidence, personal trust in someone.'

The ambiguity is especially manifest in the usage of the verb, since the term 'to believe' may stand for 'to have belief' or 'to have faith' i.e. 'to trust'. Since there is no English word 'to faith' it becomes necessary to be clear as to how the verb is being used in any particular context. The problem is complicated by the fact that the noun 'faith' is also used in different ways, and is sometimes equivalent to 'belief'.

DISTORTIONS OF FAITH

2. The Bible demands belief. The church demands belief. Neither the belief that the church demands nor the belief that the Bible demands can be produced by an act of will. I cannot simply by willing it bring about a condition of faith. But it is strange to speak of bringing about a belief by an act of will. Some things we find very difficult to believe. We cannot bring about beliefs by practicing. Nor can you bring about faith by willing to have faith. Alice discovered that she could not by trying believe 'six impossible things before breakfast'.

For faith to come into being, the person must, of course, believe certain things, for example that Jesus lived and died. But that that is not 'faith'. One may believe that it is wrong to lie. That belief will lead to actions that you might not otherwise perform.

We should not assume that 'belief' is identical with faith.

While it is not easy to speak of faith in general terms, as if there were such a thing as 'general belief', we can try to understand the different meanings involved. (1) Belief can mean *what* we believe, the content of the belief, e.g. I believe that today here and now it is Friday (2) Belief can also mean the attitude or mental state involved in believing. To believe is to have a particular mental outlook which entails a disposition to act in a certain way. If I believe that the cakes are about to burn, I shall (very likely) act in a certain way, for example, take them out of the oven. (3) The distinctive meaning for Protestant Christianity is the use of the term as equivalent to 'faith'.

It is possible that we recognise that there is not enough evidence to make a belief certain, and decide to believe anyway. In traditional Catholic theology, God moves the will to accept what the church teaches. So the action of the will accomplishes what the intellect cannot do.

Neither commands on the part of the Bible or the church can create faith. Nor can we reach the truth of faith by producing arguments and adhering to authorities. Nor can the will to believe create faith.[34]

How then does such faith come about? Is there anything to do to render it possible? Are any decisions needed? The answer is that one can put oneself within the context of faith, within the context of 'believers', within the context of witness. But there is no inevitability that produces faith even within that context.

There is all the difference in the world between the giving of assent to a proposition and the commitment in trust to a person even if I have to do the former to achieve the latter. Faith is not, in its centre, assent *assensus*. This does not, of course, mean that there is no intellectual content, no intellectual apprehension connected with the act of faith. When we say that faith is not intellectual assent, we intend to deny that in its essence, in its distinctive nature, it is not constituted as an intellectual act. So to construe it is to misconstrue it. It is to fall for the 'intellectualistic distortion of faith'.[35] There is intellectual content to an act of love But love is not in itself essentially intellectual. Thus to construe it is to misconstrue it. So with faith.

Faith is not to be confused with assent to propositions of creed, theology or Scripture, for these are some of the objects which have been made the basis for this substitution of assent for faith. Faith is not merely belief in authorities, or in the pronouncements which come to us through such authorities. Intellectual certainty is often at best endowed with a high degree of probability, or at worst with a very low degree of probability. It may be necessary to make up for the lack of probability by asserting the nature of the authority more and more strongly. 'Because it is said so by so-and-so [here insert your authority] it must be true' even if it appears untrue to reason or unsupported by evidence. But faith is not of this nature. Faith is not a matter of higher or lower probability. The certitude

---

34 Cf. Paul Tillich, *Dynamics of Faith*. New York: Harper, 1957, pp. 35-38.
35 Cf. Paul Tillich, ibid., pp. 30 ff. and Chapter II 'What faith is not.'

Justification by Grace Through Faith

of faith is not that of a higher or lower probability. The certitude of faith is not 'the uncertain certitude of a theoretical judgment'.[36]

3. Nor is faith the one work which is acceptable to God. Our previous emphasis upon faith as a gift, and as an event possible only as God himself draws near to man through the revealing Word, which is himself, has led us to repudiate any kind of independence of faith from God. Faith is not a human work, and therefore however unique it may be, is no work that God can accept. We have not fallen for a different kind of worksrighteousness when we claim that while works are of no avail for man before God, since the initiative must always be with God, nevertheless God's righteousness is revealed to man as faith is present. Faith is not at all to be construed on the analogy of the works which have been rejected. If so it will have to be rejected too. It is possible, as we have pointed out, to construe faith as assent to a dogma or creed, or ecclesiastical or Biblical pronouncement. If this misconstruction takes place, faith so misconstrued may indeed be viewed as a work, as the one work which is meritorious. Then a twofold error has been committed. Faith has been wrongly characterised in the first place; and in the second. the wrongly understood characterisation is made the basis for fideism, for fideistic legalism, for a fideistic works-righteousness.

This was what took place in Protestant Scholasticism. Faith became turned in upon itself. There was more concern for the precise definition of faith than concern for the object of faith. In this way theology became a 'faithology', a theology of subjective human experiencing.

4. We now make explicit a further denial we have already insisted upon. Faith is not a praeterrational experience which issues from the natural man. It is neither the mystical vision, in which man is, so to speak, connected immediately with the depths of his own spirit. Nor is it the 'experience' of the subject as of the ego

---

36 Ibid., p. 35.

alone, with no object. Faith 'has nothing to do with the pushing the reality of faith out of the object of faith into the believing subject'.[37]

The transposition may seem subtle. But when it takes place, we have left the world of the Bible, the concrete Hebrew-Christian world of Scripture for the world of the rationalist or of the mystic.

NO WORD, NO FAITH

We have already spoken of the 'prevenient grace of God'. That is one theological way of stressing the awareness that faith is no human creation by man, on the basis of his inner resources, out of materials that are part and parcel of his make-up as a human being. Faith is not a natural resource. It is a gift. This has also been expressed by the concept of the analogy of faith. This expression has been employed theologically in two different ways: (1) as a principle of biblical interpretation. The Bible is to be interpreted by the analogy of saving faith in Christ. Thus a canon of judgment is provided enabling us to distinguish that which is more or less pertinent, more or less edifying, more or less at the centre of the message of the Bible. A principle of canonicity is provided.[38] (2) as a means of emphasising the dependence of faith upon the gracious acts of God's revelation. It is thus linked to the revealing word which is spoken by God. Had God not acted, spoken his word, faith would be impossible.

> There is a permanent relationship between faith and the Word .... Take away the Word and no faith will then remain .... In understanding faith it is not merely a question of knowing that God exists, but also — and this especially — of knowing what is his will toward us. ... we hold faith to be a knowledge of God's will toward us, perceived from his Word.'

Calvin then attempts to specify the content of this revealing Word that precedes and produces faith,

---

37 K. Barth, *op. cit.* I/1, translated by G.T. Thomson. Edinburgh: T & T Clark, 1960, p. 268.
38 Cf. Alan Richardson, *op. cit.*, pp. 184189.

Justification by Grace Through Faith

> 'For this Word is not merely a general knowledge of God's will, for 'it is after we have learned that our salvation rests with God .... that we are attracted to seek him .... the knowledge of God's goodness will not be held very important unless it makes us rely on that goodness ... '

It is then that Calvin is prepared to give his definition of faith.

> 'Now we shall possess a right definition of faith if we call it a firm and certain knowledge of God's benevolence toward us, founded upon the truth of the freely given promise in Christ, both revealed to our minds and sealed upon our hearts through the Holy Spirit.'[39]

Thus where there is no Word there is no faith. The divine and creative grace of God calls forth the response of faith. Thus 'the human act of faith is the analogue of the divine act of revelation.'[40] When God's Word is effective in man, the presence of faith is the outcome. The presence of faith is thus evidence of the accomplished work of God's revelation.[41]

WHAT FAITH IS

Faith is

1. An act of acknowledgment. It is made at a particular time, by a particular person, 'a concretely fixable temporal: the act of this man's or that'.[42]
2. The event in which God becomes and continues to be the object of relation. God gives himself to the one who has faith. The relation is not natural nor inevitable. Neither the object God, nor the relationship of trust is created by faith. Man does not create the God in whom genuine faith is placed. The relation is asymmetrical not symmetrical. Faith is genuine in that it is God who is believed in. God is not constituted by

---

39 *Institutes.* III. ii. 67.
40 H. V. Lovell Cocks, *op. cit.*, p. 75.
41 For further elaboration cf. Karl Barth, *Church Dogmatics* I/1, pp. 260283.
42 Ibid., p. 263.

man's faith. Faith is a determinate act of acknowledgment, not any kind of trust. 'Faith is a recognition of the fact that God manifest himself in Jesus Christ not, a vague emotion in us.' (Niesel).
3. Dependent, and
4. Instrumental. Faith is dependent on the Word of God, not created, so to speak, out of its own resources. 'Without the Word there can be no faith.' Faith does not exist in its own right. It has no autonomy. If cut off from its object it dies an immediate death, or to change the metaphor somewhat, it undergoes a radical metamorphosis. Faith is independent of inborn or inherited characteristics and possibilities in man'. Sinful man cannot believe and yet he does believe.
5. Inclusive: of assent, of obedience and thus of 'works' of faith.
6. Trust: the reliance on the reliability of the other: the placing of the self in the hands of the other inevitably and irrevocably.

Old Testament teaching

Relationship to God, in trust and in obedience is a central theme in the Old Testament, but it is not expressed by the use of the term 'faith'. It is expressed in other ways. For the Old Testament the man of faith is the man of steadfastness. To believe for the Old Testament is to hold on with tenacity and persistent confidence to the object. A person 'has faith' if he holds on to God securely. But in the Old Testament it is not, characteristically, the deeply personal conception which is found in the New Testament. For it is only in Jesus Christ that the Word of God has become fully personal. So in the passage which Paul quotes in *Romans* 1:17 from *Habakkuk* 2:4, the meaning is that in all his troubles the righteous man would 'come through', that faith is the instrument for the divine protection of the righteous man'. The prophet found consolation in the fact that through confidence in God he is preserved in times of danger and crisis. Faith is a manifestation of righteousness. For Paul faith is the condition and instrument of righteousness. In both cases it is the centrality of faith that is being stressed. As the

Justification by Grace Through Faith 65

Babylonians sweep down upon the nation, the righteous man will find assurance and confidence in his fidelity, his faithfulness.

Another decisive passage was that in which the faith of Abraham is presented as influential upon his offspring. This became the subject of Jewish speculation, whose results Paul inherited. *Genesis* 15:6: 'And he believed in the Lord; and he counted it to him for righteousness.' To believe in God is to have confidence in the promises he has made.

We may contrast the attitudes of the man of faith and the faithless man: the steadfast man. and the unstable man, by quoting the words of *Deuteronomy* 28:64-67 with *Isaiah* 26:3,4.

> 'And the LORD will scatter you among all peoples from one end of the earth to the other; and there you shall serve other gods, of wood and stone, which neither you nor your fathers have known. And among these nations you shall find no ease, and there shall be no rest for the sole of your foot; but the LORD shall give you a trembling heart, and failing eyes, and a languishing soul: your life shall hang in doubt before you; night and day you shall be in dread, and have no assurance for your life. In the morning you shall say, 'Would it were evening!' and at evening you shall say, 'Would it were morning!' because of the dread which your heart shall fear, and the sights which your eyes shall see.' 'Thou wilt keep him in perfect peace, whose mind is stayed on thee: because he trusteth in thee. Trust ye in the Lord for ever, for in the Lord Yahweh is everlasting strength.'

Since God has acted in history for the sake of his people there is an appropriate attitude on the part of man that corresponds to this action. That is the attitude of confidence. Obedience is the proper response of faith.

Emil Brunner gives the following summary of the Old Testament understanding of faith:

1. Faith does not have the dominating position in the Old Testament which it is given in the New. This is because there the fact of God's self-manifestation has not yet become fully

personal. 'The historical and personal have not yet become one.'
2. Faith is a reality which determines the existence of man as a whole. Man lives in his faith.
3. Faith has a thoroughly personal meaning. It is response on the part of the person to the divine act of self-manifestation.
4. Because God manifests himself in acts, in history, man's attitude to this revelation is to be one of obedience and trust, mingled with fear of reverencing God as Lord.
5. In the creation of faith, the initiative comes from God.[43]

Faith in the New Testament

In the New Testament the term 'faith' has several meanings. In any specific case the particular meaning must be decided from the context. However, there are certain recurring meanings of the term.

Faith means the faithfulness of God, as in *Romans* 3:3.

Faith means the teaching of faith, i.e. the doctrine believed. What the apostles taught and the church believed is called 'the faith'. *Galatians* 1:23 'He is now preaching the faith which he once destroyed' *I Timothy* 4:1,6. Christians are 'nourished on the words of the faith and of the good doctrine which you have followed' *Jude* 3,6. They are to 'contend for the faith which was once delivered to the saints.'

Faith is the Christians' way of life, their life-style, the existence of Christians 'in Christ', in which they have the knowledge of God (*pistis Iesou Christou*).

Faith means trust, the relation of the believer in submission to God.

Faith means the Christian religion, the visible historical fact of the Christian community. It has come into being and continues to be.

---

[43] Cf. Emil Brunner, *Dogmatics. Vol. III. The Christian Doctrine of the Church, Faith and the Consummation.* Translated by David Cairns and T. H. L. Parker. Philadelphia: The Westminster Press, 1962, Chapter 12, pp. 152 ff.

Justification by Grace Through Faith

In short, faith is the happening in which God becomes known. In the event of faith, God is known.

The Johannine and Pauline writings in particular expound the distinctively New Testament concept of faith. It is upon these data that our attention will be focussed in the examination of the evidence.

To introduce the Pauline materials we shall quote the summary by C. H. Dodd of the meaning of faith for Paul.

> 'For Paul faith is that attitude in which acknowledging our complete insufficiency for any of the high ends of life, we rely utterly on the sufficiency of God. It is to cease from all assertion of the self, even by way of effort after righteousness, and to make room for the divine initiative .... It is an act which is the negation of all activity, a moment of passivity out of which the strength for action comes, because in it God acts ... a radical trust in God the Allsufficient, leaving no place for human merit of any kind.'[44]

In contrast to the striving for fulfilled life by means of deeds of law, and the piling up of merit through the obedience to a set of injunctions, Paul presents the simple act of reliance upon God as the only means to life. One way is a blind alley. What is closed to the legal striving is opened to faith. For there are only two ways. The former is a culdesac. 'Now it is evident that no man is justified before God by the law; for 'He who through faith is righteous shall live', but the law does not rest upon faith, for 'He who does them shall live by them' *Galatians* 3:11.

While faith is a reposing upon God, through Jesus Christ, there are not two objects of faith but one. Faith in Jesus Christ is not an additional kind of faith that supplements faith in God. Faith in Jesus Christ is faith in God. The life of the believer is 'hid with Christ in God', *Colossians* 3:3. So a song of triumph is appropriate, 'But thanks be to God who in Christ always leads us in triumph ....' *II Corinthians* 2:14. The revealing of the activity of God is

---

44 C. H. Dodd, *The Epistle of Paul to the Romans*. London: Hodder and Stoughton, 1954, pp. 15-16.

apprehended in Jesus Christ through the instrumentality of faith. 'But now the righteousness of God has been manifested apart from law ... the righteousness of God through faith in Jesus Christ for all who believe' *Romans* 3:21, 22.

The phrase 'in Christ' expresses the distinctive Pauline presentation of faith as a faithunion with Christ. The Christian is described as 'putting on' Christ. He then exists 'in Christ'. 'Put on the Lord Jesus Christ' *Romans* 13:14. For Paul the fact that faith exists means that the subject of faith is 'in Christ'. To be 'in Christ' means obedience to a new way of life. It means taking the same attitude Jesus did to sin. 'If any man is in Christ he is a new creature' *II Corinthians* 5:17. To be in Christ is to share the experience of Christ: *Colossians* 3:3,4; *Romans* 6:5. To be 'in Christ' is to know both death and resurrection. Such knowledge of God is mediated to the believer through the Spirit. *II Corinthians* 1:21.22; *Ephesians* 1:13.14. We do not have in this expression a mysticism that is a higher stage of Christian experience.

What we have is a description of faith itself through this expression. To have faith and to be in union with Christ is one and the same thing. 'Christ liveth in me. 'I live in faith', are not two phenomena but descriptions of the same phenomenon. *Galatians* 2:20. What has to be insisted on, against an interpretation that finds a Pauline mysticism at this point, is that we are dealing with a relationship term. The relationship with Christ is the one central relation of the believer. It is in virtue of this relationship that all Christian activities take their rise. 'Faith is the whole man in action as the obedient, loving son of the Father; it is what it does, or — must we not say? — what Christ does for us and in us.'[45]

If the central theme for Paul be conceived as the way to salvation as he approaches the question of faith, for John the central description is of faith in relation to salvation itself. Note Bultmann's observation, 'For John the central topic for discussion is not what it is for Paul: what is the way of salvation? For John, the central

---

45 Cocks, *op. cit.*, p. 185.

topic is salvation itself.'[46] There is agreement that salvation is 'by faith alone' but the antithesis between faith and law is not made in John, nor is there the exposition on grace, as is found in the Pauline writings. Rather faith is related to the knowledge of God. In fact in John, faith is knowing. To believe in God is to know God. Now this knowledge of which the Johannine writings speak is not some special state that is a 'higher' spiritual condition than faith. Faith knows. Faith knows God — or rather it is through faith that the knowledge of God is given. So for example, the acknowledgement of the demand of Jesus as the Christ is presented both in terms of believing and of knowing, 'and we have believed, and we have come to know that you are the Holy One of God' *John* 6:69; cf. *John* 17:21,23: 'that the world may believe that thou hast sent me.... that the world may know that thou hast sent me.' The same parallelism is found in a similar statement, cf. 17:8.

The relationship between the believer and Christ ' knowing Christ' is paralleled by the relation of Jesus to the Father. The Son knows the Father. The relation of Jesus to the Father is always described by *John* in this manner, rather than in terms of 'believing', cf. 10:15, 17.25.

This believingknowing relationship issues in obedience and love. *I John* 3:23. To know whether we 'know' Jesus Christ we may observe whether we are keeping 'the 'commandments'. *I John* 2:36. The love that God manifests to us in this relation is evident in the love the believer bears to his fellow. *John* 13:34. This is chief of the 'commandments' that Jesus has given us.

Finally, a word with reference to the presentation of faith in the book of *Hebrews*. Here the same word is used but a shift of emphasis has taken place. Roughly speaking, in *Hebrews* 'faith' is what Paul calls 'hope'. It has its eyes upon the future in view of the promises of God, as Abraham had his eyes upon the future in view of God's promises to him. Stephens translates *Hebrews* 11:1 as follows, 'Now faith is a firm confidence with respect to the objects of hope, an as-

---

46 Rudolf Bultmann, *Theology of the New Testament*. II, translated by Kendrich Grobel. London: S.C.M. Press, 1958, p. 75

sured conviction of the existence of invisible realities.'[47] He further portrays the difference in emphasis between Paul and the writer of the epistle to the Hebrews as follows. Paul arguing against putting confidence in legal works, insists upon trusting in Christ alone for salvation. Our author, seeking to strengthen a weakening hold upon all spiritual truth, aims to make the invisible and supernatural in general seem more real and practical to his readers.

Thus the Christian is called to heroism in face of the many noble examples which have through their faith demonstrated a noble courage. Jesus Christ was perfected through sufferings, and is held up as the final example of what it means to be victorious. He is the 'captain', 'pioneer', of our salvation, and he was heroic in his contest with sufferings. The Greek term *archegos* can mean 'the one who leads the way', as does a captain in the thick of the battle, or it can mean a progenitor.

---

47 George B. Stephens, *Theology of the New Testament*. Edinburgh: T & T Clark, 1931, p. 515.

VIII 'BY FAITH ALONE'

THE MEANING OF THE EXPRESSION

The next obvious move is to answer the question: What does it mean? What is this *sine qua non* of the Gospel to which the expression points? Since there are three words in the expression, we could consider each one at some length: but the decisive word for the understanding is the word 'alone', assuming that faith is to some extent understood. Since the preacher cannot assume anything, we shall look at that word too: and this will lead us to speak of the little preposition 'by' also, for a brief moment.

MANY OTHER THINGS

How can the Protestant Christian meaningfully and apparently inevitably say 'By Faith Alone'? The question is complicated because in every religion, the Christian being no exception, a great many things are comprehended, many things other than faith. In the Protestant Christian religion, it is a genuinely difficult thing to get at faith because there is so much else. Here one has to look in order to see, to dig in order to find the hidden treasure. For religion is *a way to act*, and propounds ways to act: Do! Do not! It sets out rules for the regulation of many relations of its members, defining the proper relation between church and world. A whole body of Christian ethics grows up.

It is *a way to worship* and recommends often with stubborn insistence, correct forms of worship, prescriptions for ceremonies, particular hymns, particular prayers, particular ways of saying prayers, etc.

Religion is *a way to think* recommending and often enforcing ways of thinking. Dogma and theology can often become very complicated, the despair of the theological student to say nothing of the layman. The stubbornness with which such intricate ways of thinking are pressured upon the believer witnesses to the seriousness with which particular ways of explanation are regarded.

The Christian believer has to consider all of these: acting, worshipping, thinking, and often becomes onesided because he does not consider them all. There are so many, many things connected with the church. What could be possibly meant when Paul, Luther, and others voice the slogan 'By Faith Alone?'

PAUL'S STATEMENT

In *Romans* 1:16,17 Paul claims that God's righteous activity is made manifest in the Gospel and that the just live *by faith*. Having provided an argument to that effect in the first three chapters of this letter to the Romans he then makes a summary statement at the end of his line of argument:

> therefore we conclude that a man is justified by faith (*pistei*) without the deeds of the law.' *Romans* 3:28.

Thus faith is 'without deeds'. As far as justification is concerned faith is without deeds. A later passage reads, '...the law worketh wrath; for where there is no law is there is no transgression. Therefore it is of faith, that it might be by grace ....' To translate that passage literally: 'the law worketh wrath ... therefore of faith that (*hina*) by grace.' (*Dia touto ek pisteos hina kata charin*) *Romans* 4: 15,16. Paul is here deliberately playing down everything else so as to give faith the sole place of prominence. The conclusive formula is 'Therefore being justified by faith ....' Martin Luther was in the spirit of Paul in coining the formula 'by faith alone'. So we turn now to the observations he made on his translation of *Romans 3:28* in which he had inserted the word 'alone' to produce the phrase 'by faith alone'.

LUTHER'S STATEMENT

> 'In *Romans* iii, I know right well that the word *solum* was not in the Greek or Latin text .... It is a fact that these four letters sola are not there .... At the same time ... the sense of them is there and ... the word belongs there if the translation is to be clear and strong .... I was not only relying on the nature of the languages and following that when, in *Romans* iii, I inserted the word *solum*, 'only', but the text itself and the sense of St. Paul demanded it and forced it upon me .... But when works are so completely cut away, the meaning of it must be that faith alone justifies, and one who would speak plainly and clearly about this cutting away of all works must say, 'Faith alone justifies us, and not works The matter itself, and not the nature of the language only, compels this translation.'[48]

The criticism Luther is here answering is that he had inserted the word '*allein*' into his translation of the Greek text. The German text of Romans 3:28 reads, 'So halten wir nun dafür, dass der Mensch gerecht werde ohne des Gesetzes Werke, *allein* durch den Glauben.' (Translation: 'For we therefore hold that man is justified without the works of the law, by faith alone.') What could it possibly mean? Anything? Is it another example of the vivid, concrete way of speaking of Luther?

There is another phrase like this one, *sola fide*, with a similar sound to it. It is the phrase *sola scriptura*, sometimes rendered as 'The Bible and the Bible only'. That also is a Reformation theme and these two formulae are sometimes said to express the 'Protestant principle'. There are other things beside faith and Scripture in the Christian activity. These formulae are a kind of shorthand whose meaning is quite clear when properly understood, but open to the danger of misunderstanding when taken wrongly.

---

48 'On Translating: An Open Letter'. *Luther's Works*. Vol. 35. Edited by E. Theodore Bachmann. Philadelphia: Fortress Press, 1970, pp. 188-9, 195.

'The particle 'alone' *(sola, allein)* can only be properly understood when one knows what is meant to be excluded, and in what respect. It would be nonsensical to regard the Reformation slogan 'through faith alone' as excluding works. *Works are only excluded from that on which before God I may depend.* Similarly, it would be nonsensical to regard the Reformation slogan of 'Scripture alone' as allowing, say, the minister to give up reading theology with a good conscience, or as forbidding the pious Christian to read any other literature, on pain of a bad conscience. Rather, the principle of Scripture is intended simply to exclude, but to exclude absolutely, any other witness in the matter of faith as binding save that which appeals to Scripture and submits to its scrutiny.'[49]

'Alone' could be taken to mean what it was never intended to mean. Many another theological expression has met that fate. Part of the reason for the need of an ongoing theology is that misunderstanding and oversimplification are always possible and need correction.

'Alone' does not mean that there is nothing else, (1) that there is no other object of the Christian religion but faith. 'By faith alone' does not express a fideism that denies God in the name of faith by making faith and not God the object of concern. Nor does 'alone' mean (2) that faith is the one work which is acceptable to God. The recognition that appeals to works is present under some guise or another. But the acknowledgement of faith as the sole instrument of acceptance is the decisive step to the repudiation of works as a means of salvation. But works can be relied upon incognito. There is the danger and the threat. When faith is made into a work and not even recognised as such — how could it be? — then the threat is made a reality. 'By faith alone' does not mean 'By one work alone, that work being faith'. (3) that faith is dissociated from the life of the church, and the means for communicating and nurturing faith within the church: Scripture, preaching of the word, sacraments; the Church's work in and for the world. (4) that that there are no

---

49 Gerhard Ebeling, *op. cit.*, p. 34.

works. 'By faith alone' is not an expression which excludes, but includes. There are the works of faith alone, and there are the works of law, works alone. Works are exclusive. Faith is inclusive.

When a person is justified by faith we may distinguish a twofold acceptance before God. One moves from unfaith to faith. That is to say, from a state of alienation from God, one comes to a state of acceptance with God. That is one meaning of justification by faith. There is another. For during one's lifetime one needs justification. After one begins one's life of faith one still needs justification. According to John Calvin there is a justification in which God accepts the works which he has enabled the believer to perform. He wrote, 'We must always remember that God accepts believers by reason of works only because he is their source and graciously, by way of adding to his liberality, deigns to show acceptance toward the good works he has himself bestowed.'[50]

Thus all is from God's grace and Calvin believed that this recognition of a double acceptance with God harmonised Scripture passages which appear to contradict one another on the matter of works. What about sin after the initial justification by faith. One needs further justification. So God grants it to us by his grace. The sort of thing he has in mind is the passage which seems to speak of man's good works as gaining him favour with God. He quotes *Acts* 10:34,35. 'In truth I find that God accepts no one person over another. But in every nation he who does righteousness is acceptable to him' (*Ibid.* III. xvii. 4: Calvin's translation, translated into English). Whatever God accepts from us, we have received from God's grace.

'Now in the sixteenth century Luther rejected the post-Augustinian structure of theology with its delicate and precarious balance of philosophy and theology, reason and revelation, created and uncreated grace, divine transcendent cause and infused *habitus*. Thus the pressure of theology and the need of his own soul moved him toward the crisis of a '*novum et mirum vocabulum* (new and wondrous vocabulary)'.

---

50 *Institutes*, III. xvii. 5.

IX JUSTIFICATION

Relationship with God

The doctrine of justification is concerned with the 'problem of the presupposition and the possibility and the truth of the positive relationship of God with man, of the peace of man with God'.[51] With this doctrine, as with many others, the precise words and concepts which are used are of great importance. It is a matter of the form of expression. A slight, or an apparently slight, turn in the road may lead us a long way away from the goal in sight. The same terms may be used but may come to stand for opposed realities. When this takes place we have antagonistic theologies opposed to each other, but employing the same terms.

Vocabulary

Historically, the protest of the Protestant Reformation was centred around the concepts of 'justification', 'grace', and 'faith'. These terms became the meeting place of the opposed systems. For the Reformers, the task involved a rejection of the medieval significance that had been given to the key terms, and a reformulation of them, that they felt was more consonant with the message of the New Testament and the truth of man's experience as he stood *coram Deo* (before God).[52]

---

51 Karl Barth, *Church Dogmatics*, IV/1, p. 528.
52 G. Rupp, *The Righteousness of God*. London: Hodder and Stoughton, 1953, p. 101.

FIDUCIA AND OTHER TERMS

Christian faith, *fiducia*, is trust in and commitment to God as he reveals himself through the Word spoken about Jesus Christ. The term *fiducia*, trust, draws the contrast between faith and various forms of belief It distinguishes faith from assent, *assensus*, the act of acknowledging something to be the case, often because it has been proposed by authority. When the evidence is strong enough, we usually assent. The term *fiducia* distinguishes faith from *notitia* which means 'noticing', 'having something brought to one's attention', 'being aware of', 'awareness'. Faith is a conscious act. That means we give our attention and consideration to what is involved. Some subject matter has come before our attention. We are aware in the act of faith.

Other terms point out the particular nature of Christian faith. *Implicit faith* is dependent, second-hand belief. It is the acceptance on the recommendation of someone else. *Explicit faith* is the result of a process of personal decision. It follows the weighing of the evidence. It is an involved conviction regarding propositions we believe.

Another important distinction is between *fides quae creditur*, the belief, the accepted doctrine, literally, the faith which is believed, and *fides qua creditur*, trust, commitment, personal involvement, literally the faith by which it is believed. Both of these sets of terms insist on the important distinction between mere acceptance and self-involved trust.

THE CHURCH AND THE COVENANT

The act of God creates the possibility of man's salvation. It is God's act in Jesus Christ that makes possible the instrumentalities through which the reconciliation now becomes possible, becomes an actual reality for the believer: i.e. the church. No-one is saved outside the church. But the church is the creation of God, consequent upon the saving act of God in Jesus Christ. The church is the locus where the saving activity of God, which broke into the world decisively in the Christevent, is continued within the world. The church is the means through and the place at which the reconciliation effected for us, becomes the reconciliation effected in us. Through it the completion of God's act made real for us at the Incarnation, is made real in us through the Spirit. It is an interesting question where the boundaries of the church are to be drawn.

The covenant conception is thus not superseded in the New Testament. God's activity for men is not a haphazard one, thrown out at any point in the stream of world history. It is tied to the covenant and it is creative of covenant. It is through the covenant, and for the covenant people that Jesus has become the Christ.

CHRISTUS PRO NOBIS, CHRISTUS IN NOBIS

In Jesus Christ a change of status has taken place. God has come to be present among men in the Christ-event, and the world is different as a consequence. The world has been reconciled to God. This is the way the New Testament writers put it. On the basis of the accomplished reconciliation the plea is made that men themselves become reconciled to God. 'You have been reconciled! Be reconciled!' These are the two themes which run parallel whenever the act of God in Jesus Christ is presented. God has acted. That is the first and final word. Receive the benefits of that act: that is the proximate word. God who has already acted to redeem and reconcile the world without you, will work in you too to accomplish his purpose of reconciliation there. There is the work that God does apart from us, and there is the work that God does within us. But only the believer says this.

The distinction has been clearly made in Protestant theology between these two moments in reconciliation. They have been described as the *Christus pro nobis* and the *Christus in nobis*, i.e. *Christ for us* and *Christ in us*. What God has done apart from us is of no avail unless he also accomplished something within us. What he accomplishes within us is related to what he is and what he has done apart from us.

Justification and the Judgment of Sin

When man is justified, God also is justified. The justification of man is also the justification of God. The fact of sin, rebellion, stands between man and God and calls for this act of God, if man is ever to be in relation to God again. Thus God's justifying act in Jesus Christ answers two questions: Can man find a gracious God who pardons his sin? Can man find a place where his sin is judged so utterly and yet find release from that judgment? Can we indeed at the same time speak of God as both 'gracious' and 'right', 'just'? Is there a point at which man may be utterly condemned and yet utterly pardoned? Is there an act which at the same time manifests both God's utter graciousness, and also his radical condemnation of man's sin? How can God who is holy and man who is utterly sinful can be reconciled? How may there be peace between a holy God and sinful man, accomplished in a way that is right, i.e. just? Since man's sin is directed against God, is rebellion against him, is negation of his will, peace will mean God's negating man's rebellion without ceasing to maintain his case against man, in all its rigour. It is Luther's question, 'How may I find a gracious God?'

The Christian answer is that such a God is found in Jesus Christ. Now it is a temptation in theology to stress the benefits of Jesus Christ, and that is right and good that this should be done. But the starting place must be with incarnation. God became man. But man stands under the judgment of God. In whatever ways the manhood of Jesus is unlike ours or like ours there must nevertheless be directed against the man Jesus Christ all the judgments of God in their most intense form without reduction if there is to be a crucial dealing with sin. If the sin of man can be focussed in this man, if the anger of God can be directed against the sin so focussed in this man, may there not be a reprieve, a probation, for other 'men'? Can there be a point at which the 'summing up' of man's rebellion and God's judgment and grace meet? Can it be that there is a place where the judgment of God is executed against man and yet this act be the supreme act of grace? Only if God himself be

Justification by Grace Through Faith

the initiator and be himself the Victim. The Christian answer that must take precedence is the answer given in the fact of Atonement.

It is of course a paradox, rising to the point of absurdity: that one who is sinless and thus no mark for the judgment of God might be identified with the sin from which he is free. Moreover that he be God: that is unthinkable. Unthinkable, precisely! And it is especially unthinkable when put in judicial terms. The sinless one is so identified with the sinful that he is numbered, reckoned among the sinful. *Luke* 22:37 records Jesus applying to himself the words of *Isaiah* 32:2: 'For I tell you that this scripture must be fulfilled in me. And he was reckoned with transgressors, for what is written about me has its fulfilment.' 'The immense paradox of the Christian Gospel of forgiveness is nowhere more shocking than in this judicial metaphor.'[53]

As the cross is followed by resurrection so Jesus Christ is delivered from the abandonment which he underwent for the sin which he had become ('he hath made him to be sin for us …' *II Corinthians* 5:21). 'My God, why hast thou forsaken me' (*Mark* 15:34) is followed by 'being by the right hand of God exalted'; 'Him hath God exalted with his right hand to be a Prince and a Saviour' (*Acts* 2:33, 5:31). The Cross and the resurrection are aspects of a single event in which the righteousness of God is manifested and in which the reconciliation of man with God is made possible. The divine approval is given to the act of Jesus Christ. His obedience is acknowledged. His sacrifice is accepted, the saving consequences of the act are now brought into operation. God manifested that he was in the right in relation to his creature. It was of God's grace that this manifestation was made. It was life and not death, fulfilment and not extinction that God willed for the creature. It was these that were made known in open manifestation through the resurrection. It is through this act that God's right was manifested. Had God destroyed the creature, had God permitted him to verge into the nothingness when he had chosen, that too would have been right.

---

53 So comments J.S. Whale, *Victor and Victim*, Cambridge: The University Press, 1960, p. 48.

But it would have been a right within God alone, known only to him. That this was no theoretical possibility is evinced by the cry of dereliction from the Cross, 'My God, my God, why hast thou forsaken me?' *Mark* 15:34.

'COUNTED RIGHTEOUS' OR 'MADE RIGHTEOUS'?

It is sometimes customary to make a distinction between the Protestant and Catholic doctrine of justification on the basis of a difference between imputation and impartation. When the Protestant is justified, he is counted as if he were something he is not. When the Catholic is justified he is made righteous. With the former the believer is accepted for nothing which he may do. In the latter case, he is accepted as he has become holy. We should ask: Is this distinction a valid one? Does the Protestant say that a man is accepted for what he is not? In the desire to lay all the stress upon the grace and mercy of God is it in fact necessary to deny that righteousness is in no way man's when the act of justification takes place? Does the grace of God, received by faith make no difference not simply to the status of man, but to the man himself? May we say that the distinction between standing (status) and being (character) is a false one? Is it the case that one is accepted by God, not *because* (except in a very carefully defined sense) but *in that* he has come by grace to have faith? If faith is a reality does this not certainly distinguish one from the person of unfaith that one was?

THE ALTERNATIVES?

1. that God's righteousness is infused into man, so that man comes to partake of the divine nature.
2. that this process takes place by assent to dogma or to the directives of the church: i.e. that faith is 'belief' *assensus*.
3. that the righteousness which is God's attribute of 'justice' ensures that man shall be accounted just before God, since he has faith, whereas he is not actually righteous.

Justification by Grace Through Faith

4. that the man actually becomes just before God, and thus is accepted for what he is, a man of faith.
5. that while one does not become righteous before God, nevertheless one is received for one's faith, be it assent or trust.
6. that God's righteousness is his saving grace in activity and that through faith one becomes the object of that grace, is placed in a saving relation to God, who saves man not for what he is but purely because God is gracious. The faith through which one comes into relation to God has no status independent of the initiating grace of God.

The following are some of the issues involved: the meaning of 'righteousness' as it refers to God and to man; the meaning of faith; the definition of the priority of God's grace, his saving activity, his 'righteousness' to any of man's responses; the status of man's acceptance of God's righteousness; the resultant status of man before God, whether it be any different from the state of nonfaith, now that he has come to have faith; the relationship of righteousness, faith and the grace of God to the manifestation of God in Jesus Christ.

So we may draw the conclusion: the expression 'righteousness by faith' is a kind of shorthand which, if properly understood, sets forth in an epigrammatic and cryptic form the meaning of Christianity. Since it is in such form terse and symbolic (the great creeds of the church were called 'symbols' for good reason), it may easily be misunderstood, as indeed may other expressions used in connection with it (for example, 'by faith alone'). So there is need for clarity. What is the nature of the faithapprehension of this reality? How shall we best conceptualise what we experience and produce an adequate theology of salvation.

A LEGAL FICTION?

The essential problem is as to how we shall talk about faith. The desire of those who say that in justification one is only accounted righteous by a kind of sleight of hand by God by which he engages in a 'fiction', is to preserve the ultimacy of grace from beginning to end. How may we preserve this ultimacy and speak satisfactorily? To address ourselves to this matter we must clarify the various ways of conceiving the relationship between grace and faith. We shall see grace as the personal movement of God to the sinner, who in his helplessness cannot assist himself and faith as the response we may make to God's grace unavailing itself. All is of God's grace, the faith through which man is justified included. Faith results from this personal activity of God. It enters into the very fabric of a person's being, into the depths of the person and produces a change from what was before — a person of unfaith. Now that one through the initiating grace of God, has come to believe, one becomes a different person. Through faith one is in right relationship to God, whereas before one was not. The difference is fact not 'fiction'. That term appears in a well-known comment on *Romans* by Sanday and Headlam.

> 'The righteousness of which St. Paul speaks though it issues forth from God, ends in a state or condition of man the believer, by virtue of his faith is accounted or treated as if he were righteous in the sight of God ... the person so 'accounted righteous' may be, and indeed is assumed to be, not actually righteous but an offender against God. There is something sufficiently startling in this. The Christian life is made to have its beginning in a fiction.'[54]

What we must object to is the fiction, the 'as if'. We must be extremely careful how we say. God looks at us 'as if' (we were not sinners). The comment we are considering regards the expression in such a way that it results in saying that God is made to engage in a piece of legal bookwork (something like counting magnitudes as if they were zeros while knowing that they are not). How can this be a manifestation of justice in the narrower sense of the word?

We must note that while the ungodly are the ones who are justified — and who else? The healthy do not need a physician.

---

54 W. Sanday and A. C. Headlam. *The Epistle to the Romans*. International Critical Commentary. Edinburgh: T and T Clark, 5th edition. 1902, p. 36.

Justification by Grace Through Faith

But not all the ungodly are justified. The preceding verses indicate that the apostle is concerned with the completely gratuitous nature of the process by means of which one is accepted by God. The one justified is an object of the grace of God. We have previously stated that God's action in his movement towards men is neither accidental nor arbitrary. The ungodly are not justified in either an accidental or an arbitrary manner. The ungodly who are justified are those who have faith. Faith distinguishes between two classes of the ungodly.

> But the admixture of personal terminology, e.g. faith and grace, with legal expressions e.g. justification, debt, works, law, lends itself to unclarity and to possible distortion of intended meaning. We may well be admonished by the following warning: 'any scheme of ideas that clusters round a legal or rabbinical conception of God's relation to man ... must fail to do justice to the spiritual fact of forgiveness ... Any such terminology could only be a partially opaque medium for St. Paul's real message ... To believe in God from the heart is to be pleasing to him to satisfy him, to be right with him, ... the phrase ('declared righteous') has its own importance and value as a repudiation of 'worksrighteousness', yet also we may feel that we desiderate a more purely personal mode of denoting simple, loving forgiveness .... *Justificatio*, forgiveness is not immoral, but it requires more than moral terms for its expression.'[55]

So from a purely legal point of view the action of God in justifying man is immoral. It is a breach of strict justice and could easily be interpreted to open the way to a looseness and licence which could condone all sorts of evil deeds, and no good deeds at all. If we are aware that the use of such terms inevitably lands us in paradox, we shall not be unduly distressed, but sympathetic in our interpretation of them.

The concept of justification has had an important history in Christian thinking. It is, as providing the means of expressing a

---

55 Mackintosh, *op. cit.*, p. 117.

doctrine, one way of expressing the act of God in Jesus Christ as it becomes mediated to the one who has faith. But it is by no means the only way of expressing this fact. It does not have exclusive claims to the attention of the theologian therefore. One thing must be said. If said in this terminology it must be said along with other modes and expressions.

The terminological framework in which the doctrine of justification is expressed is one familiar to the Jew. For him the judge must be just. In this respect he is like God. A false charge is to be shunned and the innocent are to be acquitted. As to the wicked, they are not to be acquitted: 'for I will not acquit the wicked' *Exodus* 23:7. So also it is said, 'He who justifies the wicked and who condemns the righteous are both alike an abomination to the Lord' *Proverbs* 17:15. If that is a picture of what God is, it only has to be shown that man, all men are wicked and condemnation is inevitable. But that is not what is to be found in the New Testament. For there God is described as 'him who justifies the ungodly' *Romans* 4:5. Moreover St. Paul will allow no question as to the rightness of the act of justifying man. God is true if all men are false. There is an upholding, not a violation, of law. 'Let God be true though every man be false … Do we then overthrow the law by this faith? By no means! On the contrary, we uphold the law' *Romans* 3:4, 31.

What then has happened? If this is the language of the law court, it is obvious that it is a very unusual law court. 'In fact, the language of the lawcourt has been used with deliberate intent, to destroy the very idea of legalism in religion.'[56]

What actually happens in this act of 'justification'? Is it possible to specify from two angles: what God does for man, and what happens to man when the experience of justification takes place? We have already pointed to the paradoxical nature of the act of God. Once more we remind ourselves that we may speak of the possibility of justification only in terms of the actuality we have experienced. That actuality is extremely difficult to express in terms

---

56   P. S. Watson, *The Concept of Grace*. London: Epworth Press, 1959, pp. 3334.

Justification by Grace Through Faith

of law. Many different figures are employed in the New Testament to point to this reality, one that God has initiated.

What happens to man? The starting point for our discussion may well be the 'sufficiently startling' statement of Sanday and Headlam referred to above. A fiction? God playing a trick upon himself? God making believe that something is not so, for the sake of bringing benefit to man? A kind of celestial hocuspocus from which man is to receive nothing but benefit? What is fictional about the act of justifying man? The problem that this commentary expresses in this less than satisfactory way is that man who does not cease to be a sinner, is accepted and not rejected by God. Man who is sinner finds welcome at the father's house. The theological purist does not understand the first. The elder son in the parable did not understand the second. Both misunderstood the difficulty of setting forth, in legal categories that would be entirely satisfactory, the fact that God as Father is welcoming home the lost boy. But we stay with the legal categories and see what may be said. It is important to notice that the legal form is one among several others. If we learn from the New Testament, this will mean that we have an example for our own theology. We should find many ways of expressing the Gospel appropriately.

Can we admit that it was right to justify the ungodly? The Jew could not. Such an expression is actually used by Paul in *Romans* 4:5 where God is described as the one 'who justifies the ungodly *(ton dikaiounta ton asebe)*'.

This is the tenor of the decided rejection of the several objections in *Romans* 3:118. Here it is pointed out that God is faithful, just and true; that God's rightness in justifying the sinner by no means leads to immoral consequences, to libertarianism; that before God there are no righteous men, not even Jews, except as God justifies. His conclusion is that 'God is righteous and that he justifies him who has faith in Jesus' verse 26. The same objection was made against the acts of the Son: if he eats with publicans and sinners, he must himself be a sinner. To befriend sinners must be to partake of their sin. So runs the argument. It leads to the questions: 'If Jesus deliberately cultivates the friendship of publicans and sinners, must he not be a sinner himself? If God 'justifies the ungodly' 'how can he be righteous himself?' Watson, *op. cit.* p. 35. The Cross is the answer. There God's initiative is seen. There, God goes into successful action against the sin of man. God himself is the answer to the problem of forgiveness.

We may set forth the situation as follows: Either man does something that leads to the realisation of fellowship with God: or God himself does something to create such fellowship. God could have recourse to various possibilities: overlook sin; leave man to himself; take man's sin upon himself. The first would be the unjust way, the unethical way. The second would leave no man to be worried with the problem at all. The third way is what God did — the way that is called 'right' in the New Testament. By means of it God can be both just and justifier.

God forgives the sin that is seen to be serious. God forgives the sin to the penitent. Man must repent. Justification is no glib and costless act in which the seriousness of sin is repudiated. In the act of justification, sin stands out in all its seriousness. It is seen to be exceedingly sinful. It is such only to the eye of faith. It is in the act of faith that the best of any human accomplishment is seen to be nothing before God. It is here that the believer stands by faith alone. It is here that God justifies by grace alone. God reveals his grace. Man responds in faith. Justification issues as the result.

SIMUL JUSTUS ET PECCATOR

It is therefore obvious from what has been said that there is no playing down of the heinous nature of the reality of human sin. Forgiveness deepens the sense of sin. It does not dissipate it. Sin is known in all its intensity when grace is known in all its fullness. These are seen in the moment of justification, as they have been seen in the cross. Thus it is the sinner who finds forgiveness. It is the sinner who is justified. He does not cease to be sinner. He is now a forgiven sinner. The forgiveness is no fiction. It transcends the acts and concepts of the law court. The state of being still sinner is no

Justification by Grace Through Faith

fiction either. What seems fictitious from a legal point of view is that the two should be put together and the sinner be forgiven, be justified. Luther powerfully expressed The paradox in his dictum *simul justus et peccator (at the same time sinner and righteous)*.

Some representative statements from Luther will make the intent of this maxim clear.

> 'The saints are intrinsically always sinners. Therefore they are always extrinsically justified; but the hypocrites are intrinsically always righteous, therefore they are extrinsically always sinners .... we are extrinsically righteous in so far as we are righteous not in and from ourselves and not by virtue of our works but only by God's regarding us so .... the saints... are sinners in fact, but by virtue of the reckoning of the merciful God they are righteous; they are knowingly righteous and knowingly unrighteous, sinners in fact but righteous in hope .... God ... takes us at the same time for sinners and non-sinners. Sin remains and simultaneously does not remain in us.'[57]

The paradox we here encounter is well expressed in the words of the hymn by Frederick W. Faber:

> 'There's a wideness in God's mercy
> Like the wideness of the sea.
> There is kindness in his justice
> Which is more than liberty.'

If God's reckoning is a reality and not an unreality, something like the above must be said. For if God regards us as so, must it not be so? Is not God's activity creative activity? The God who created light is the God whose light is manifest in his other creative act, Jesus Christ. So says *II Corinthians* 4:6 Justification is a creative act of God. He 'speaks' and it is done. He who is accounted righteous is righteous. For if he is righteous he may be accounted righteous. He is righteous because God has accounted him so. He is accounted righteous because he has no righteousness of his own. It is faith that

---

57 Martin Luther: *Lectures on Romans*. Library of Christian Classics Edition, translated by Wilhelm Pauck, Westminster Press, 1961, pp. 124 125.

makes the difference. The man of faith is no longer identical with the man of unfaith. A decided distinction must be made. The unrighteous man is the faithless one. The righteous is the one of faith. But, and it must be emphasised, one is righteous *by* faith. *Faith is the instrumental reality.* It does not create the state of justification, any more than it creates the religious object. *It is the vehicle* through which the reality is made known, when in the freedom of his love he wills to make himself known. The creative activity of God in love toward the sinner is called grace. Grace produces the faith. Faith responds to grace. Grace produces that which is reckoned to faith. All is of God. By God's reckoning we become what we have not yet been. In faith we are righteous because God has reckoned us so. As righteous we are also sinners, *simul justus et peccator.*

The Protestant regards the act of God's righteousness which issues in the justification of man as coming at the beginning of the Christian life. There is no need for a life time of the performance of works in order to reach the state of acceptance by God. The corollary of the assertion that 'a man is justified without the works of the law' (*Romans* 3:28) is that justification is an instantaneous act at the beginning of the Christian life. I have been accepted, and therefore I may be assured of acceptance. God has accepted me. I must accept the acceptance. In Thomas Aquinas, the architect of the theology of the medieval church, justification comes at the end of the life, and is never assured. The assurance will only come at the close of a long series of activities. At the very best 'this knowledge (i.e. of grace) is imperfect even if possible'.[58]

The stress must be laid upon the priority of God's grace. Justification, acceptance of man by God, has its basis in the grace of God and hence grace must be the primary term all the time. The doctrine of justification by faith is not primarily concerned with faith, but with grace. The source and thus the resting point of justification is outside of ourselves. God in Jesus Christ is the source of faith and he is gracious quite apart from my attitude toward him. Thus the expression 'by faith' might be misleading. For faith

---

58 See Pegis, *op. cit.*, p. 680.

Justification by Grace Through Faith

has its source in grace. It derives from God. So we will go badly wrong if we should say 'by my faith' and not 'by God's grace'. Faith by its very nature directs us away from ourselves outward toward God the source of all good, and the fountain of all forgiveness. We would do better to use the preposition 'through' rather than 'by' in describing the experience of acceptance with God. We would then talk of justification through faith. For indeed the clause is an abbreviation of the longer and clearer one: *Justification by Grace through faith*. Faith is the instrument through which grace flows to man, the channel cut by the flow of that grace, so to speak. Thus faith is directed away from itself towards its source in God. So the preposition of instrumentality, in Greek *dia*, German *durch*, and English *through* is appropriately used to qualify 'faith'. Not 'by faith' but 'through faith' is the correct way to speak. But if we understand that this is what the expression '*by* faith' means then its familiarity need not mislead us.

> 'We are not saved *propter fidem* but *propter Christum*; not *by faith*, therefore, but *through* faith (*per fidem*) .... We are not saved by faith, as though our faith as a 'work' of ours could make us righteous before God by outweighing our sin and imperfection .... Faith receives him before it receives his righteousness. Faith which is only the instrument by which righteousness is received, cannot without absurdity be confounded with Christ .... Our faith is at best weak and wavering; if it must be the ground of our justif8ication then we are lost indeed .... By virtue of this atoning work of Christ our faith becomes possible .... After all, it seems, we *are* justified by faith; but it is Christ's faith, not ours, that is the ground of our justification.'[59]

If all is of God, we must insist upon the fact that faith is the instrumental reality. We must insist upon it so strongly that we modify the slogan, 'justification by faith', so as to correct a misinterpretation which would shift the centre of Christianity away from its source in Jesus Christ.

Paul Tillich issues the salutary warning:

---

59 H. F. Lovell Cocks, *op. cit.* pp. 140-141, 142, 145.

'Not faith but grace is the cause of justification, because God alone is the cause. Faith is the receiving act, and this act is itself a gift of grace. Therefore one should dispense completely with the phrase 'justification by faith' and replace it by the formula 'justification by grace through faith.'[60]

It is a warning we do well to heed.

Tillich puts the matter in his own terminology as participation and acceptance of the New Being.

THE ESCHATOLOGICAL ELEMENT IN JUSTIFICATION

Vincent Taylor pointed out that in the doctrine of justification 'eschatological ideas are transmuted and brought into the present.'[61] We do not have to wait until the last trump to know what the verdict will be. The mercy of God is exhibited on the sinner's behalf here and now. This means that the final judgment is robbed of its terrors, terrors due to not knowing the outcome. We know before what the outcome will be. Justification is the transition to acceptance by God from a state of alienation from him. For the fourth Gospel judgment is a present fact. Here and now men enter into eternal life. The future is the consummation of this. He that believeth on the Son hath eternal life. *John* 3:36, 6:40. So the passage in *Revelation* 22:11 indicates that when the last judgment comes the time for amendment is over. The judgment is there pronounced upon what man then is. This is determined by what he now is. If he is justified now, he does righteousness. If he is not justified now he does not do righteousness. Rather he does unrighteousness. The Judgment is pronounced upon what man is. What a man is now is determinative of what he then will be.

---

60 *Systematic Theology. Vol. III*, Chicago: University of Chicago Press, 1959. p. 224.
61 *Forgiveness and Reconciliation*. London: Macmillan, 1946. p. 50.

Justification by Grace Through Faith

'RIGHTEOUSNESS OF GOD' IN LUTHER

The conception became the focal point of Luther's spiritual difficulties. So he wrote,

> 'For I hated this word (he refers to *Romans* 1) 'Justitia Dei', which by the use and consent of all doctors I was taught to understand of that formal or active justice (as they call it) with which God is just, and punishes unjust sinners .... I did not love, nay, rather, hated this just God who punished sinners and if not with 'open blasphemy' certainly with huge murmurings I was angry with God .... I began to understand the Justice of God as that by which the Just lives by the gift of God, namely by faith .... that passive justice   with which the merciful God justifies us, by faith, as it is written, 'The just lives by faith .... Afterwards I read Augustine ... where beyond hope I found that he also similarly interpreted the Justice of God: that with which God endues us when He justifies us .... The justice of God is that by which we are made just by his gift ... Justice, i.e. grace. This word I learned with much sweat ... Justice is that which the Father does when he favours us, with which he justifies, or the gift with which he takes away our sin.[62]

Luther knew that God's justice condemned sinners. He knew this from the law. If that was what the Gospel taught then there was no difference. It was the realisation of this that created the deep spiritual crisis in Luther's experience. 'As Holl suggests, Luther's problem lay, not in how to combine 'the divine justice with the mercy (*misericordia*) or the goodness (*bonitas*) of God but in the conception of justice itself.' the problem was solved when Luther came to see that *justice is not simply a divine attribute but a divine gift to men*. In the reconception that dawned upon Luther there emerged 'the fountain of a new doctrine of God'.[63]

So Mackintosh describes justification as follows, 'Justification is not an attribute of God towards the sinner or a divine judgment

---

62 Quoted in Gordon Rupp. *Op. cit.*, pp. 122123, 124, 126.
63 Ibid., pp. 127, 128.

regarding him; it is the completion of a process of grace by means of which the sinner is actually made into a righteous man'.[64] He then makes three important points concerning the teaching of the Reformation (Luther).

1. A man is not made righteous by moral rejuvenation. God deals with him as a righteous man, in virtue of his faith. 'He certainly is not made righteous by any grace that acts magically upon the soul's substance; but none the less justification in the Lutheran sense is *effective as well as declaratory.*[65]
2. Faith for Luther is 'not correctly to be described as but a condition of being justified or accounted right with God ... Faith itself is righteousness.'[66]
3. Faith is for Luther naturally and inevitably productive of good works. Since it renews the heart, we say far too little when we talk of obedience following from it as if by an interval; obedience is as vitally and indissolubly united to faith as breathing to life or body to soul.'[67]

If we construe justification in purely forensic terms we shall misconstrue it. But we must also avoid the opposite error, for in denying such forensic interpretation we may tend to make the effects of justifying faith into the ground for pardon.[68]

What Luther reacted against

Religious movements do not take place in a vacuum. Antecedents are challenged. Tendencies are picked up and appropriated. Reactions occur and take account of the antecedents and the tendencies. We misinterpret if we construe justification in purely forensic terms. 'In protest against barely forensic notions, a *tendency*

---

64 *Op. cit.* p. 131.
65 Ibid., p. 149.
66 Ibid., p. 150.
67 Ibid., p. 151.
68 Cf. Ibid., p. 154.

Justification by Grace Through Faith

arose to turn the moral quality and effects of justifying faith into the ground of pardon.'[69]

To make this concrete we shall now make a brief survey of the thought of the church preceding Luther concerning the questions of pardon, merit and grace.[70]

The New Testament teaches that God for Christ's sake freely pardons the sinner who repents and who has faith in his mercy. The sinner is accepted for what Jesus has done and not for anything that he can do, for being a sinner, he can indeed do nothing. Forgiveness, justification, is the free gift of God, the state of man making it impossible that there should be anything for which God may be in debt to him.

Gradually this liberating conception of God's activity became distorted as it was misunderstood in the apostolic fathers. The concept became associated with erroneous conceptions as the centuries passed, until the medieval church was raised upon a perverted conception of grace, faith, and justification. We now trace in broad outline certain lines of development, in their turn leading to the understanding of the medieval church whose teachings Luther challenged.

The first stage was a misunderstanding of the great truth that the grace of God which was manifest in Jesus Christ was given freely, without any consideration of merit on the part of the recipient. What was required for the New Testament writer was faith only. But immediately the great truth is misunderstood, and while there are expressions which suggest that God's love is freely imparted to the penitent, there are alongside of these such expressions that, referring to works as they do, cancel them out.

So Clement can write in *I Corinthians* (96 A.D.):

> 'And we therefore, who by his will have been called in Jesus Christ, are not justified of ourselves or by our wisdom or insight or religious devotion or the holy deeds we have done

---

69 Ibid.
70 Cf. H. R. Mackintosh, *op. cit.* Chapter VI, pp. 125ff.

from the heart, but by that faith by which almighty God has justified all men from the beginning.'

Even if we may feel that the last clause sets aside the distinctiveness and hence the centrality of the Incarnation and the Cross it is clear that the writer is attempting to portray the Pauline doctrine of faith. But other passages are quite different:

> 'Because of her faith and hospitality Rahab the harlot was saved.' Further: 'Since then, we are a holy portion, we should do everything that makes for holiness .... We should clothe ourselves with concord, being humble, selfcontrolled. far removed from all gossiping and slandering, and justified by our deeds, not by words.'[71] So in a standard edition of Clement, the following judgment is made: 'Clement, then, took over justification by faith, but quite failed to appreciate what was meant. We may suppose him to be typical and that the Epistle was thus interpreted by the church to whom it was sent.'[72]

The *Didache* (*The Teaching of the Twelve Apostles* is variously dated. By some it is placed within the first century.) In it we hear of 'payment'.

'If your labour has brought you earnings, pay a ransom, for your sins. Do not hesitate to give and do not give with a bad grace; for you will discover who he is that pays you back a reward with a good grace.' 'If you can bear the Lord's full yoke you will be perfect. But if you cannot, then do what you can.'[73]

The writer recognises the capacity of man to do what will put God in his debt. The idea of the two ways, the way of life and the way of death, is presented not to emphasise the utter need of God's grace, but to make an ethical contrast, and to admonish the believer to apply himself to the task of walking in the right way. To do so will be to have God as one's debtor.

It is hardly too much to say that, even in its noblest representatives the motto of the Early Church is 'salvation by faith and

---

71 For the quotations see 32,4; 13.1; 30,1,3.
72 Clark, *I Corinthians*, p. 27.
73 *Didache* 4.6-7, 6.2.

Justification by Grace Through Faith

good conduct' and the predominant point of view is that sins are forgiven on the basis of amendment .... salvation is the prize and recompense of a perfect moral life, to be achieved out of one's own resources.[74]

So we come to Tertullian (A.D 160220) who determines to a large extent the thinking of the next period of the church's thought, and who exercises great influence in later centuries, both in reference to Christology, and also with reference to a doctrine of penance. He has been called 'the Father of Western Christianity'.

The most permanent influence of Tertullian was his interpretation of the Gospel. God is the lawgiver. Man's job is to keep the law. We must do this on pain of death. But man is sinful, and by sinning has incurred God's guilt. When we sin, we must render satisfaction to the person against whom we have sinned. If we sin after baptism we must make retribution to God for that sin. For Tertullian, religion was a legal relation between a lawgiver and a subject. One must keep the law; if one fails one must pay fines for breaches. It is better to pay the fine now than to be punished later. If now we keep the law, we are alright. But we may do more than the law requires. If so we put God in our debt. So he distinguished between the normal requirements and the councils of perfection, by means of which one can store up merits. So he wrote, 'The affliction of the flesh is the victim that placates the Lord by means of the sacrifice of humiliation'.[75] Satisfaction precedes pardon.

For Tertullian, grace is understood 'in essentially impersonal terms as a supernatural, yet quasimaterial, substance or energy .... It is a fact that from Tertullian onward, grace — at any rate saving grace — tended to be thought of as a more or less impersonal power imparted through the sacraments.' Tertullian's conception of the relation between men and God is thus fundamentally legalistic and the conception of grace is adapted to fit this scheme .... Paul ... opposes grace to law and works, as Tertullian does not.[76]

---

74 Cf. H. R. Mackintosh, *op. cit.*, pp. 126-127.
75 *De Patientia*. 13.
76 P. S. Watson, op.cit., pp. 76, 77.

SUMMARY

We now make a summary statement as to the meaning of justification. Justification means:
1. that God is for man and not against him. This cannot be taken for granted,
2. that man is sinner, does not know it, and cannot help himself,
3. that God judges man in his sin and that God forgives him of his sin,
4. that this forgiveness is a real and not a 'fictional' ('as if') passing over of sin,
5. that in justifying man God is right, not arbitrary or capricious. God is righteous.

Justification thus has to do with God who is gracious and with man who is sinful. Justification concerns both *dikaiosune pisteos* and *dikaiosune theou* (*Romans* 3:26). But 'the righteousness of faith' is 'the righteousness of God'. For to speak of faith is already to acknowledge the operation of grace. God's grace is always prior.

X THE WORKS OF FAITH

❛The glory of God does not consist in receiving something from us which will make him richer! It consists rather in giving us the means of being no longer nothing.'[77]

In the act of justification, since it is primarily God's act, a gift is given which must be received. The receipt of a gift calls for an attitude different from that of receiving wages for labour done or for goods delivered. The requisite response is different because the event is different, and because the source of the event is different. 'Now to one who works, his wages are not reckoned as a gift but as his due,' *Romans* 4:4. And the attitude of faith is one that keeps on receiving, one that keeps on taking what God gives to man. That is the humiliating thing about it. That makes us all like dependent children, who get everything and give nothing. All is by faith. Since justifying freedom, sanctifying grace, calling and final bliss are all by faith alone, i.e. are all due to the grace of God alone, the requisite attitude is always demanded. The Christian can never get past the state of openness, humble willingness, unconditionality, a recognition of his unacceptability. Such are constantly required, and unremittingly present in the life of the Christian. There is no point at which reliance is upon any other than God. There is no point at which reliance is through anything other than faith.

---

77 Quoted in E. L. Mascall, *He Who Is*, London: Longmans, 1962, p. 169.

'Acts' and 'Works'

Thus there are no 'Works'. There are no appeals to 'law'. But in what way, in the act of justification does faith exclude works and in what way does grace supersede law? Is there nothing to be done? Is not the believing something that has to be 'done'?

The one justified has acted and will do many acts from now on. Acts that are done in faith, inspired by God's grace, are not 'works of law'. The way of faith and the way of law are two opposed avenues. Must we not speak therefore of acts that must be done while at the same time denying that such acts that have to be done are by no means 'works'? What is it that distinguishes what must be done from a work of law? In short, what is a work of law?

At this stage we get help from Dietrich Bonhoeffer and from the Book of *Galatians*. We run the risk when emphasising the importance of faith of developing a quietistic attitude which finds no place for any talk of doing, or of works at all. At worst this becomes what has been called an attitude of 'solifidian sloth'. That is the lazy side of it. The activistic distortion of this point of view is the view sometimes called libertarianism. If you have faith, it does not matter what you do. That can easily become: do anything and you will be alright. The opposite danger is that of replacing faith by works — works of any description. Paul is concerned with this latter danger in *Galatians*. Bonhoeffer is concerned with the former danger in *The Cost of Discipleship*.[78]

Excursus on Galatians

In the second chapter of *Galatians*, it is a question of two kinds of works: circumcision, and a deliberate restraining from association with the Gentiles. The first chapter sets forth clearly the basis of Paul's preaching in the Christ-event, the revelation of God. (See our earlier discussion.)

---

78 Bonhoeffer is concerned with the former danger in *The Cost of Discipleship*. Translated by R. H. Fuller. 6th edition. London: S.C.M. Press, 1959.

The personalities concerned in the two test cases were Titus who was not circumcised, and Peter who wavered in his attitude to the Gentiles. In his visit to Jerusalem Paul was urged to consent to the circumcision of Titus. He refused. What was at stake was no less than the freedom of the Gospel, 'the truth of the Gospel' *Galatians* 2:5. What Paul was demanding was more than merely verbal assent to his doctrine of freedom in Christ.

One work, any work, was useless, in fact a hindrance, as far as faith was concerned. Titus was the test case. Paul won the victory he anticipated. Titus the test case was the standing example that the Gospel of Jesus Christ did not require works, and that the Jerusalem brethren had accepted the position. Titus had not been circumcised. That being so, circumcision or any other comparable act, or for that matter any act at all was out of the question as far as salvation was concerned. This was a standing illustration of Paul's insistence that the Christian gospel means 'Jesus only', and not 'Jesus and...' some work or other. 'Jesus only' is the way of faith. 'Titus they did not compel to be circumcised' (2:3). 'Jesus and ...' some work or other, is the way of law: 'there are some who trouble you and want to pervert the gospel of Christ' (1:7).

The same point was at stake in the encounter of Paul with Peter. The basic contention was: If they have been justified by faith, Gentiles do not have to live like Jews. For Jews seek justification by works. It is the same principle Paul expounds by recourse to this incident (cf. 2:16). From Paul's own experience of intimate union with God through faith in Jesus Christ only, following as it did upon the experience of futility and religious frustration through the way of law, Paul states succinctly what the two ways involve, and provides the religious basis for his rejection of the 'Jesus and ...' alternative. The objection which he meets, as stated in 2:17 is that if a disregard for the statutes of the law is maintained, Christ is made a 'minister of sin', an instrument of further and further sinning. Therefore such preaching must be wrong. Paul's rebuttal is an incisive one. He answers in short. But who is the transgressor? If one insists upon an obedience to the statutes of the law as a means to justification, i.e. acceptance with God, that one is the transgressor.

Paul is not simply throwing back upon the head of the objector, without reason, the charge that is hurled at him. *He is calling for a complete reformulation of the problem.* Such a reformulation would show that the conclusions the Jewish, legalistic objector was drawing were by no means valid. Paul is here contending: Your definition of sin is wrong. As a consequence, your definitions of righteousness and law are also wrong. You draw the false conclusion that in Christ law is violated because you have identified a particular conception of law with the will of God. But, Paul argues, you can break the law, as understood by the Jew and not be a transgressor, not violate the will of God. In fact Paul contended, you have to violate 'law' as the Jew sees it, in order to do the will of God. *hamartoloi,* i.e. violators of what to the Jews is 'law' are not guilty of *hamartias,* i.e. they are not sinners in the sight of God. They are not violators of the will of God.

The tradition-bound Jew could not abandon his deeply entrenched concepts. But because sin is defined concisely and emphatically does not mean that it is being defined correctly. Emphatic statement does not mean correct statement.

So Paul insisted that there could be no reversion to the old type and retention of the benefits of salvation. If I go back to the things I have once destroyed, I repudiate the experience of justification and with it the grace of God (verse 18). What Paul had abandoned as a way to acceptance with God were the statutes of the Jewish law. He had seen that to break what the Jew said was sinful was not to commit real sin. Paul had thus repudiated law as a way to God. He had repudiated obedience or attempted obedience to some demand or other as a way to peace and acceptance. He had repudiated a way of life based on law. The rejection of that way of life meant for him the reorientation of his whole theology. The futile attempts at keeping law had shown Paul the real inadequacy of law as a road to God. It was futile to go along that road of human effort to attain salvation. The law, the legalistic interpretation of Moses, had

Justification by Grace Through Faith

shown its impotence to save him. He turned from the way of law to Christ. For Paul obedience to the Mosaic law, interpreted legalistically as by the Pharisees, had showed to him the invalidity of the way of law as a means of grace. He could only abandon that way, if salvation was to ensue. He is related to it no more. He has broken off all relations to it. If Paul was to 'live to God' (verse 19), he had to abandon such a way. 'Subjection to law in reality prevented the unreserved devotion of the life to God — this is the one vice of legalism, that it comes between the soul and God, interposing law in place of God.'[79]

BONHOEFFER: DISCIPLESHIP IS NOT 'CHEAP GRACE'

Bonhoeffer's concern is with the fideism that cheapens the grace of God, that makes discipleship a thing of no cost. He opposes talk of grace that can speak of discipleship without the cross, because it can speak of it without obedience. He rejects the thinking that argues that since grace is free, it can be had, everything can be had, for nothing. In short that grace is cheap, so cheap that sin can be justified without the justification of the sinner. Against this Bonhoeffer insists, 'Only he who believes is obedient, and only he who is obedient believes.'[80]

What is then important is the assertion that obedience is necessary from the conclusion that it is therefore a work that is acceptable to God, on the strength of it being that work. That would be the opposite error. If we perform the work which has to be done for the sake of obtaining faith and grace, already we are in bondage to that work. The work has to be done however. But it has to be done in the right attitude: looking away from itself as a work; looking to the Lord who calls us to do it.

> 'If we think our first step is the precondition for faith and grace, we are already judged by our work. and entirely excluded from grace .... Nevertheless the external work must be done for

---

[79] Ernest De Witt Burton, *The Epistle to the Galatians*, Edinburgh: T. and T. Clark, 1975, p. 134.
[80] *Op. cit.*, p. 54.

we still have to find our way into the situation where faith is possible .... We can only take this step aright if we fix our eyes not on the work we do, but on the word with which Jesus calls us to do it .... The step of obedience must be taken before faith can be possible .... Do not say you have not got faith. You will not have it so long as you persist in disobedience and refuse to take the first step. Neither must you say that you have faith, and therefore there is no need for you to take the first step.'[81]

OBEDIENCE

What then is the nature of genuine obedience? It is here not a matter of good intentions and well-meaning response. What is being obeyed and how is the obedience being rendered? If there is to be genuine obedience, it will be response to God. That means it will be response to exclusive and absolute demands. Now absolute demands are not to be identified to the relativities of a situation, or to negations made on the basis of such relativities. For the tendency is to confine obedience easily to certain specific and manageable injunctions, or to easily mastered negations. However the series of such injunctions and negations tends to become more and more complicated as more and more new situations must be brought within their compass. Inevitably if this takes place the vision is restricted to the area that is mapped out by such injunctions or negations. The rules become allimportant.

We could take for example the commandment to keep the Sabbath holy. That command might be so elaborated that it becomes 'Thou shalt be found in attendance at the meetings available on the Sabbath, or to at least two of them.' The demand for goodness becomes 'Thou shalt not put on cosmetics.' 'Thou shalt not view a film in a commercial place of entertainment,' and so on. But a relative demand is one that can be escaped by justifying the proviso that is so essential (for these good reasons....) on this one occasion to violate the rule. But genuine obedience to an absolute demand leaves no part of life untouched. The demand is not now

---

81 Ibid., pp. 5,57.

confined to the maintenance unscathed of rules few or many. It is the persistent, application of that demand into every area of life. and this is much more encompassing than confining 'faith' within the limits of a set of rules. It gives its own directives and creates its own rules. We may not relativise the absolute demand in order to escape it.

As a matter of fact we do not need grace for the fulfilment of rules of our own making. The rules that we make for ourselves are usually within the bounds of our own possibility. But never can we perform unaided the absolute demand of God. Our righteousness is insufficient for 'except your righteousness exceed that of the scribes and Pharisees ye shall in no wise enter into the Kingdom of God'. That the more exceeding righteousness has not yet been attained may indicate that it is indeed an absolute demand that we are asked to obey.

Genuine obedience has God for its object, and faith for its instrument. Which is once more to say that which has been insisted upon so often: righteousness by grace through faith.

Is there not at the root of a claim to the grace of God on the basis of works an arrogance that finds selfsatisfaction in the particular works we are doing? We claim that we are obedient and think that our claim to God's mercy is dependent upon the obedience which we have rendered. The result is hypocrisy. For God does not accept any work which does not have its source in him. In this matter it will be hard to give up the long-accustomed habit of an insincere obedience. For that requires nothing beyond the reach of our purely human powers, and makes it possible for us to be satisfied with what we do and lets us rest upon our labours. So in thinking that we are obedient we become proud, and in our failure, which is disobedience, we find selfsatisfaction in the works we may do.

XI SANCTIFICATION

SUMMARY STATEMENT

'At the same time sinner and righteous.' This is the description of the sinner who has been justified which we have accepted from Luther. We may say then, apparently paradoxically, that man is both righteous and is also accounted righteous. He is righteous by virtue of God's reckoning of him, in that God does not count his sins against him. He is a man of faith. But he is a faithful sinner. Sanctification is the state in which he now exists. He is holy. The reality of sin becomes a diminishing reality. The reality of righteousness becomes an increasing reality. But, since quantitative terms are objectionable we shall instead replace these by others. Let us say then that the righteousness becomes the dominating quality and the sinfulness the retreating quality. Man's sinfulness expresses itself less and less in acts of actual sinning. Man's righteousness, graced to him by God, expresses itself more and more in acts of faith, until finally faith has overpowered sinfulness and he has become, by God's grace, a person in whom, ideally, the only acts which he performs are acts which spring from faith and manifest the righteousness of faith. This is what is meant by sanctification.

SANCTIFICATION

When justified, the believer becomes a saint. To continue to believe is to continue to be a saint. Faith is an event. It is a continuing event. A virile faith is a nurtured faith. The reality which faith is, the faith that justifies is a living faith, a progressing reality.

There we said that the sinner becomes a saint. But the term 'becomes' can mean different things. A caterpillar becomes a butterfly. When this takes place it ceases to be a caterpillar. A complete metamorphosis has taken place. What existed no longer exists at all. The continuity is not in the least obvious. But the rich man can become the poor man not ceasing to be a man. Which meaning of the word 'becoming' fits the description of the change at justification? There are, it seems, three possible alternatives: (1) the believer arrives at conversion, the becoming is a being; (2) the believer never arrives but is always only reckoned as having arrived. The becoming is not realised at any point; (3) the reckoning is the arriving, but the arriving is a movement: the being is becoming.

The Christian is one whose being is a becoming. The life of the believer after justification is not what it is if it is not in process of development. The life of faith is a life of passage. If we characterise the prefaith state as 'world', then the life of the believer is a life of passage from world into Christ: 'From ... into .... Movement away from one world into another.'

Walking

There are many Biblical figures of speech that suggest such progress. The most familiar one is that of walking. So Paul speaks of walk in newness of life' *Romans* 6:4. He can say, 'We walk by faith' II *Corinthians* 5:7; and 'As ye have received Christ Jesus ... so walk ye in Him' *Colossians* 2:6. The figure is also found in the Johannine writings: 'walk in the light', 'walk even as he walked'. *I John* 1:7, 2:6. Of those who rejected Jesus it is said, 'They went back and walked no more with him' *John* 6:66.

What does it mean to 'walk in the steps of that faith' *Romans* 4:12? Any Biblical symbol has its limitations. To press it beyond its limitations would be to distort its application. The life of the Christian is like a walking. The simile is suggestive of progress, of effort, of a goal to be attained. We may say 'steps from Christ' as

Justification by Grace Through Faith

well as 'steps to Christ'. We mean by this that there is no step at all but that Christ is the source of the walking. For how can one take a step who cannot walk? It is God who instructs us how to walk. 'It was I who taught Ephraim to walk' *Hosea.* 11:3. But the simile depicts the nature of the life of faith as a life of becoming. It is a state in which there is progress. The state of faith is one of progressiveness. The state is not static. It would not be the state is it if progress were not being made. The state of faith consists in becoming. This is the meaning of the assertion that faith is living. What is living becomes.

ORIGINAL SIN

Faith moves in the context of sin. The reality of sin is the atmosphere in which faith moves. Hence an examination of the reality of sin is essential to an understanding of the reality of faith and reconciliation. Sanctification is the undoing of sin, and man as sinner.

Sin is an affair of the whole man. It is man who sins. He cannot detach himself from his sins, for it is he who commits sin. As the whole man as a unity is responsible for his individual acts of sinning, so those acts of sinning are an expression of what the man is, manifested in the particular cases. Since man is sinful, the individual acts of sin are an expression of what he is. For what he does springs out of what he is. The expression 'original sin' was coined to express the fact that the individual acts of sin are not isolable from the whole man, that acts of sin are not accidental acts of sin, but they are veritably the expressions of what the man essentially is. When man sins, he is expressing his nature. That nature is a sinful nature. It must therefore issue in acts of sinning. What is, i.e. a sinful nature, expresses itself in ways that reveal its nature.

It is a misunderstanding to interpret the expression 'original sin' as standing for a theory of how that state of man's sinfulness came to be. 'Original sin' is the description of a condition. It is not a theory of how that condition came to be. We can recognise the condition without explaining how it is that this is the way man is.

Theories of origin always come subsequent to the recognition of what is. When we have come to recognise what is, we may then seek to explain how what is came to be. It may be important that we do. It may not. So 'original sin' is not the sin of Adam. It is not the first act of sin. It is the sin that meets us as we come on to the stage of the world's history. It is the sin that lies at the origin of all acts of sinning. It is the bitter root from which all acts of sinning spring. It is the description of a condition. It is not the name for a theory of how that condition came to be.

It is thus necessary to distinguish the *specific* acts of sinning, 'sins', from the nature of man from which they spring, 'sin'. The root problem of man is not that he commits acts a, b, c, d, etc., individual and isolated acts of sin, 'sins', but that he is the person, the kind of person that does such acts. There would be no solution to his dilemma therefore if only the isolated acts of sinning, the sins, were handled. For the acts of sin spring from a sinful nature. We are the kind of people who commit acts of sin. If we are to cease committing acts of sin, we must become different people. There is a power that lords it over us, that prevents us from becoming what we might be, what we ought to be. That power is the power of sin, original sin. Any adequate doctrine of sanctification must occupy itself with the problem of man's radical sinfulness, his nature bent away from God, and issuing in all manner of perversities, perversities that have sprung from the basic, underlying perversity that man is. For the sinfulness of man expresses itself in many different ways.

Many different expressions in the Old Testament express the many-sidedness of sin. Since the Hebrew delighted in concrete ways of speaking, these descriptions of sin are most expressive.

Sin in the Old Testament

The Old Testament uses many different words to describe sin, since there were many different ways of sinning. While there has been no consistent translation of the different terms, certain basic ideas stand out prominently.

Justification by Grace Through Faith

To sin is to disobey God. This disobedience is positive, not merely negative. Sin has multitudinous forms. Sin was primarily disobedience to God. Sin against man was a secondary conception. It was sin because God had forbidden man to injure his fellow. So different words were needed.

(1). 'Bad' (*ra'*) is a comprehensive term, as in English, meaning 'something harmful'. It is used of figs, of 'evil figs' in *Jeremiah* 24:8, of animals, of the lean 'illfavoured' cattle of Pharaoh's dream, *Genesis* 41:21, of Elisha's use of meal to counteract poison: 'And there was no *harm* in the pot'. *II Kings* 4:41. It means unfit, unpleasant, worthless, injurious. In a moral sense it means 'evil' as opposed to 'good': 'we cannot speak unto thee bad or good' *Genesis* 24:50; 'wicked in the sight of the Lord', *Genesis* 38:72 cf. *I Samuel* 17:28: 'I know thy pride and the *naughtiness* of thy heart'. So it means 'injurious' or 'morally bad', 'a breaking up of what is good and desirable'.

(2). 'Wicked' (*rasha'*) is always used in a moral sense: for example of the confusion and activity of the wicked.

But the wicked are like the troubled sea when it cannot rest, whose waters cast up mire and dirt. There is no peace, saith my God, to the wicked *Isaiah* 57:20,21, cf. *Job.* 3:17, Psalm 1:1, 3:7. The word *rasha* refers to sin against God or against man.

(3). 'The most general use of guilt ('*asham*): is of the 'trespass offering' *Leviticus* 5:1. Here it is an offering for a sin committed in ignorance which afterward comes to the attention of the offender. It is used of the state of a person who has sinned through error, in ignorance (a moral or ceremonial offence). When it has been brought to his notice the man is to bring a 'guilt offering': e.g. *Leviticus* 4:13. 22, 27, 5..2,3,5,6,17. So '*asham*' implies breach of commandment, which, when known as such, calls for atonement.

(4). 'Missing the mark' (*chata*) is used literally of slingers in *Judges* 20:16: 'everyone could sling stones at a hairbreadth and not miss'. In its moral usage, one misses the right mark because he aims at a wrong one. So it refers to deliberate, calculated sin, and is used mostly of sinning against God; e.g. of Pharaoh: *Exodus* 10:16: 'I have sinned against the Lord your God.' God's forgiveness is available for such sin: 'Though your sins be as scarlet, they shall be as snow.' *Isaiah* 1:18; 'I have blotted out as a cloud thy sins.' *Isaiah* 44:22. Moses says to the people who have set up and worshipped the golden calf: 'Ye have sinned a great sin.' *Exodus* 32:30. Cf. *Genesis* 42:22: 'And Reuben answered them, 'Spake I not unto you, saying, Do not sin against the child.' The word *chata* is regularly translated 'sin'. Throughout the Old Testament the word means basically that man comes short or fails of the aim which God intended his children to reach and so includes any departure from the law of right.

(5). The word *shagah* means to err, to go astray, to waver, to wander, to deviate from. It is used of a straying sheep in *Ezekiel* 34:6: 'my sheep wandered through all the mountains'; of the reeling of a drunken man in *Isaiah* 28:7; of accidental sin in e.g. *Job* 19:4: 'cause me to understand wherein I have erred'. In *Proverbs* 19:27 one 'errs' from the words of knowledge'. The word *shagah* is used of accidental sin. But a person is responsible for the way he goes. So in reference to sin, the term is used of an action in which the person chooses to 'go astray'. One is ignorant when one should know: e.g. *I Samuel* 26:21: 'I have sinned ... I have erred exceedingly'; *Psalm* 119:2:'Thou hast rebuked the proud that are cursed which do err from Thy commandments.' The term presupposes that there is knowledge of right and wrong. The provisions for sacrifices in daily service of the sanctuary presupposed a code detailing right and wrong. To 'err' was to commit sin unknowingly and afterwards have it brought to the attention. *Leviticus* 4: 2, 22, 23, 27, 28. So the cities of refuge were for those whose 'error' was unintended: not for those who had deliberately murdered, or used means that might lead to death. So *Numbers* 35:9‑24. (Note verse 11: 'which killeth any person at unawares' cf. v. 15).

'If all the uses of shagah and shagag be taken together, it seems clear that the Jews distinguished between innocent and culpable error, and that it was only for the latter that atonement, was required.'[82]

(6). 'Rebellion, *pasha*, means 'to refuse subjection to a rightful authority'. It is usually rendered 'transgression'. and usually used of rebellion against God. It is used in its literal sense of the revolt of Edom in *II Kings* 8:20, 22. Cf. *Isaiah* 1:2: 'I have nourished and brought up children and they have rebelled against me'; cf. *I Kings* 8:50 ' ... forgive the people all transgressions wherein they have transgressed against thee.' *Pasha is* Sometimes rendered 'sin' and 'trespass' e.g. in *Proverbs* 28:13: 'He that covereth his sins shall not prosper.' and in *Hosea* 8:1: 'They have trespassed against my laws.'

(7). 'Treachery, breach of trust. The word *ma'al* is regularly rendered 'trespass'. In two thirds of the instances it denotes unfaithfulness between men and God. It is also used of unfaithfulness between people. Aachan 'committed a trespass. *Joshua* 7:1, 22:20, i.e. deliberately broke the trust God put in him, by disobedience. Uzziah deliberately disobeyed in offering incense, cf. *II Chronicles* 26:18: '... for thou hast trespassed.' It is used of those who married heathen wives in *Ezra* 9:2,4: ' ... the hand of the priests and rulers hath been chief in this trespass.' Punishment is threatened for such sin as 'setting up idols in their heart'. *Ezekiel* 14:13, 15:8.

'The persons guilty of sin in this particular aspect were chiefly persons in authority. A certain trust had been reposed in them

---

82   C. Ryder Smith, *The Bible Doctrine of Sin*. London: Epworth Press, 1953, p. 19.

and they had abused it. Much had been given to them and much was required of them The nation of Israel as a whole were put in a position of high privilege and consequent responsibility: hence, their departure from the way of God was marked specially by this word as an act of unfaithfulness.' Girdlestone. *Synonyms of the Old Testament*, p. 82.

(8) 'Wrong', *avah* signifies 'to be bent' So it means 'perversion', 'distortion' as in *Lamentations* 3:9: 'He hath made my path crooked.' Cf. *Esther* 1:16 'Vashti the queen has not done wrong to the King only ....'

Reckoning?

The question about sanctification has been put in different ways. One way of asking it is in terms of the doctrine of justification that sees that event only as a reckoning. It runs as follows. What is not a reality but only a reckoning now becomes a reality. The critical questions then are, 'At what point does God no longer reckon us holy? At what point is the transition to actual holiness made?' If, as we have held, the becoming is a being rather than only a reckoning, the reckoning actually introducing the being, such a question becomes misplaced, and has to be reconceived. We create needless problems for ourselves if we made false steps at the outset. Such a presentation as the above can however be set within the context of grace. Such 'imparted' righteousness, it is said, is given by God, even if it becomes our own.

Sanctification and Sin

However we are closer to the biblical way of stating it, if we conceive of sanctification as the progressive continuance of the reality which begins to be at justification. What is a reality at justification continues to be. This being is a becoming. What has come to be continues to be: relationship with God, forgiveness, obedience, submission. Sanctification is the progressive continuance of what began to be at the moment of justification, in the face of sin.

Sanctification is the reversal of sin: it is its undoing. It is a process that continues as long as sin is present — which is all the time. It is a process which had a beginning when the sin was recognised along with the remedy for it, when sin was apprehended through the eyes of faith, and was forgiven. The sin with which the sanctified believer lives is forgiven sin. But the sin which needs to be forgiven is also a reality with the believer who is not beyond the possibility of sinning. Temptation is an everpresent reality. The doctrine of sanctification is the doctrine of the reversal of human sinfulness. Thus however sin is defined, sanctification will be accordingly be defined as its antithesis. If the reality of 'original sin' is unrecognised, then sanctification becomes the matter of complete perfection, of a life absolutely free from every and any taint of actual sin. It is then a most discouraging dogma.

PAUL, WESLEY, SCHLEIERMACHER

Historically, the definition of sin has been the foil against which the doctrine of sanctification has been expounded. When Paul presented sin as the lordly power that dominated man, he found the remedy in the removal of the dominion of sin, 'Sin shall not have dominion over you' *Romans* 6:14. When he presented it as the dominance of the flesh over man, he presented sanctification, as the reverse of this, as the dominance of the spirit. The reverse of carnality is spirituality, ' ... the desires of the Spirit are against the flesh' *Galatians* 5:16.17. When the way of sin is presented as bondage to the law, the sanctified life is presented as the life of freedom in Jesus Christ. So the 'law (i.e. principle) of the spirit of life in Christ Jesus has set me free from the law of sin and death' *Romans* 8:2.

Similarly John Wesley defined sin as conscious violation of known law. It was the explicit and active denial of what was known to be right. Thus sanctification was for him freedom from any known sin, any known violation of an explicit commandment. Thus, while he himself did not claim it, Wesley could emphatically commend the reaching of a doctrine of entire sanctification.

Friedrich Schleiermacher defined sin as lack or distortion of the Godconsciousness, a failure of the Godconsciousness to be in the Christian what it was in Jesus, direct and continuous. This God-consciousness he also called 'piety'. Lack of piety was the problem. That was what constituted sin. Sanctification was therefore the continuity and the dominance of piety or the God-consciousness in the life of the believer. But Schleiermacher had another way of putting the matter. He spoke of the area of 'faith' over against the area 'world'. These are the two antithetical realities. The dominance of the one means the lack of ascendancy, the suppression of the other. While world was present in church, the area in which faith was to be found, there it was dealt with, and there the ascendancy of faith over world was to be found in various individuals, at various stages of preponderance. Sanctification is thus 'severance from participation in the common sinful life'. It is 'an active tendency to a new common life'. Sanctification is thus progressive. Schleiermacher thus recognises the fact of original sin. He wrote,

> inasmuch as the sinfulness of each has a ground of existence prior to him and external to him, his sin cannot be perfectly blotted out, but remains always something in process of disappearance. In so far as it has not yet disappeared, it may make itself visible and acts will occur within the state of sanctification similar to those common before regeneration .... It is chiefly by this fact, that sin can win no new ground, that the state of sanctification is most definitely distinguished from all that went before.'[83]

Sanctification not absolute perfection

It is now time for us to distinguish more carefully between original and actual sin, so that the doctrine of sanctification may more specifically be defined. It is the sinner who comes to believe. It is, that is to say, one bent at the centre of his being by sin that

---

[83] Friedrich Schleiermacher, *The Christian Faith*, translated by H. R. Mackintosh and J. S. Stewart. Edinburgh, T & T Clark, 1960, pp. 505, 507, 508.

Justification by Grace Through Faith

expresses itself in different ways. The first fact that the believer recognises is that he is radically sinful, that there is a power that lords it over him and one he is impotent to handle. He recognises that there is good which he has never done, and that at the very heart of his being there is that which prevents him from being what he should, and hence doing what he should. It is the believer that recognises this. It is the believer that comes to find the conflict within himself — the experience of *Romans* 7 — and who finds the resolution of it in the forgiveness proffered by Jesus Christ. Faith is granted to human beings affected by sin at the heart of their pseudohumanity. It is the sinner who believes.

What then? Does the sinner all of a sudden become absolutely holy? Is the transformation so complete that one will never ever after that commit sin? Is there any point at which the believer may say, 'I have now arrived at absolute perfection.'? 'Absolute perfection' means the state of being beyond sin. The answer must be a decided negative. That is not what sanctification is. Sanctification is not complete perfection. Sanctification is believing in Jesus Christ, continued without cessation. It is a state which is a progress. Sanctification would not be the state it is were not progress being made. It is a state in which that progress is made, as the relation with Jesus Christ is sustained. Sanctification is, one might say, the natural state, is the natural condition of the Christian. As health is the natural condition of the body, so sanctification is the natural condition of the Christian. This means that sanctification is no lofty, abstract ideal that requires heaven and the hereafter, nor the monastery or nunnery for its realisation. It is the holiness that comes as the accompaniment of faith. It is, in fact, one way of talking about it, that is, the life of faith. The life of faith is the life that is sanctified. It is the life of the saint.

THE NEW TESTAMENT PARADOX

In the New Testament we find two strands standing side by side, with no attempt to harmonise, indeed it appears, with no realisation that there were any difficulties to be harmonised. On the one hand the Christian is admonished to be perfect, 'let us cleanse ourselves from every defilement of body and spirit, and make holiness perfect in the fear of God' *II Corinthians* 7:1; 'he disciplines us for our good that we may share his holiness.' *Hebrews* 12:10: 'Strive for the holiness without which no one will see the Lord.' verse 14. That is the one side: we are to be holy, we are to be perfect. The other statements present the fact of sin in the state of faith. As Christians we sin and we need forgiveness: 'If we say that we have no sin, we deceive ourselves .... he is faithful and just to forgive us our sins ....' *I John* 1:8–10; 'with my flesh I serve the law of sin. There is therefore now no condemnation' *Romans* 7:24.

In this apparently contradictory and ambiguous situation the believer is called a saint. In fact, the term 'saint', 'saints' is used 67 times in this way in the New Testament. We may say then that the one who is sanctified is one who while he believes, may nevertheless sin, and when he does commit sin finds that God is a gracious God, finds that he is forgiven from the sin committed, finds that in the relationship with God, which is a relation of humility, penitence and gratitude, the sin may be forgiven. God is a Father who loves his son. That is the discovery of faith. That is the atmosphere of faith. Sanctification is thus a state: being in the condition of faith, the condition in which when there is sin, it is set within the atmosphere of grace, of faith, and so is disposed of. But it is a state in which progress is being made. Holiness is perfected, followed after. There is progress in holiness. But at every point in that progress God's grace and man's faith meet. Acceptance and assurance result.

After a comprehensive survey of the Biblical evidence, Ryder Smith expresses it in the following manner, ' ... the fundamental concept is that Christians are 'holy' because, through Christ by the Spirit, they are in fellowship with God and therefore, in their small and imperfect way, like Him .... Through the Holy Spirit every 'saint' is beginning, in some elementary and faroff way, to be like God.'[84]

---

84 Ryder Smith, *The Bible Doctrine of Man*. London: Epworth Press, 1951, pp. 191,192.

An interesting passage relevant for our consideration at this juncture is *I Corinthians*. 6:11. It reads: 'And such were some of you. But you were washed, you were sanctified, you were justified in the name of the Lord Jesus Christ and in the Spirit of our God' (RSV).

This passage is interesting for a number of features. In the first place we have a series of aorist tenses which, as is obvious from the context, refer to an action viewed as complete. Moreover the juxtaposition of these three verbs indicates that the hard and fast distinction between having been sanctified and having been justified may be an artificial one. The different words here refer to the same event. The event which had its external counterpart in the washing of baptism had its internal basis in the passage from guilt to pardon. 'The new life is viewed here as implicit in the first decisive turn to Christ, which again was inseparably connected with their baptism.'[85] One wonders whether this is doing less than justice to the passage in question, where the terms seem to be employed as synonyms. When the designation *hagioi*, 'saints', is recalled it would not seem improper to connect the verbs as synonyms. The verb *hagiazo* would then refer to the act by means of which the Corinthians were constituted saints, the act of God's grace, received through faith.

That this is in harmony with the context is evident by a perusal of verses 9 10. Such were some of them. But the letter to the Corinthians is filled with sharp rebuke. If the Corinthians were saints, they still had far to go. What then was the difference? The difference was that they had believed. They were 'such'. They were no longer. But their conduct left very, very much to be desired. They have, as we say, a long way to go. But they began to believe and continued in their belief in Jesus Christ. It is this that made the difference and it is this that constituted them saints, having been sanctified. As long as there was faith, there was sanctification. To continue to believe

---

85 A. Robertson and A Plummer, *The First Epistle of Paul to the Corinthians. International Critical Commentary.* Edinburgh: T and T. Clark, 1911. p. 120.

is to be sanctified. For faith is relationship with the Holy God. A similar juxtaposition of concepts is found in the usage of the various nouns in *I Corinthians* 1:30: ' ... Christ Jesus whom God hath made our wisdom, our righteousness, our sanctification and redemption.' All of our righteousness and sanctification is based upon the accomplished fact of redemption in Jesus Christ. Hence the stress on redemption. The term 'redemption' (*apolutrosis*) is placed last in the sentence, which is the position when a word is emphasised. We may take 'righteousness' in two ways: (1) of the revelation of God in Jesus Christ; (2) as a designation of the kind of life that the saint will live. So righteousness is the way of life of the saint. The term points to the ethical aspects of the life of faith.

XII FAITH, FREEDOM AND WORKS

THE STATE OF FAITH

The point at which we have now arrived is quite simply that one is holy, one is perfect, as one has faith in Jesus Christ. There is no need to be anxious concerning the sins of the past for they are in God's hands — the hands of a gracious God. There is no need for concern about the future unattained perfection. That too is in God's hands. The believer keeps constantly renewing his faith in the gracious God known to him in Jesus Christ — that is sanctification.

But we have affirmed that this state is a state in which progress is being made, that it is a state which is a becoming. Sanctification as a state is also a process, a state in which there is no room for satisfaction with past accomplishments. And the greatest Christians were quite explicit that they were the greatest of sinners. Consciousness of sin in the state of faith is not a morbid, unhealthy introspection. The believer who is sanctified is, in that state of sanctification, driven to recognise his imperfection, knowing of all people not to have 'arrived'.

Sanctification is a state that is also a progress. It would not be the state it is were not progress being made. Sanctification is the description of one who really believes, one who is justified by grace through faith. Sanctification is the state which is a progress, of which justification is the beginning. Death to sin is followed by a living in faith. And in the New Testament the indicative and the imperative lie side by side.

Death imagery

'You are dead.' That is the indicative. 'Be dead.' That is the imperative. Affirming the death one has died is never over and done with. The indicative is variously expressed in the New Testament. For example, 'How shall we who die to sin still live in it?' Paul presents the figure of death, with the obvious implications that are to be drawn from it, to provide sufficient answer to the objection to his teaching that grace increases the sin of man. *Romans* 6:2. 'But now we are discharged from the law, dead to that which held us captive'; 7:6. 'For I through the law died to the law, that I might live to God' *Galatians.* 2:19, cf. *Romans.*7:4. 'For you have died and your life is hid with Christ in God' *Colossians* 3:3 Since death means the cessation of life, there should be no evidence of the past life that has now passed away. The figure can thus easily become the basis for admonition, as in *Colossians* 2:20: 'If with Christ you died to the elemental spirits of the universe, why do you live as if you still belonged to the world?' There are the clear examples of the imperative using this figure of death, as the following examples show. 'Put to death what is earthly in you …' *Colossians* 3.5; 'So then brethren we are debtors, not to the flesh, to live according to the flesh — for if you live according to the flesh you will die, but if by the Spirit you put to death the deeds of the body you will live' *Romans.* 8:13.

That the indicative and the imperative are put together in this way illustrates that sanctification is a state in which affirmation of what made that state possible, must continually be made. The imperatives remind us that we must keep on affirming the faith. The faith which enabled the believer to die must now be affirmed so that he remains dead. He can only remain dead if he constantly renews his faith. That is the state of sanctification. Obviously defection is always possible. There is no state of having arrived, no state of instantaneous perfection. It is not a matter of 'once having

Justification by Grace Through Faith

been saved, always saved'. There is always the possibility of relapse into sin. There is always the possibility of taking sin as normal, as approaching sin without faith. To ask for forgiveness means that we do not take sin as the normal thing. Its removal means humility. But the ultimatum is given by a God of mercy and love. Before him the only appropriate attitude in sin is that of penitence.

We refer back now to Martin Luther's description of the state of the man justified by faith as *simul justus et peccator*, 'at the same time sinner and righteous'. A favourite illustration of his is that of the good Samaritan. The man who fell among thieves represents the sinner. He is wounded, but on the mend. As long as he is mending he is getting well, and is therefore well. This is at times presented in another way, the illustration now being that of the convalescent. Luther asks of the convalescent, 'Is he sick or well?' And he answers as follows,

> 'He is actually sick, but he is healthy by virtue of the sure prediction of the physician whom he believes. For he reckons him already healthy because he is certain that he can cure him, indeed because he has begun to cure him and does not reckon him his sickness as death.' He applies this to the justified believer. 'Now can we say that he is perfectly righteous? No! but he is at the same time both a sinner and righteous, a sinner in fact but righteous by virtue of the reckoning and the certain promise of God that he will redeem him from sin in order, in the end, to make him perfectly whole and sound .... Though forgiveness is indeed real, sin is not taken away except in hope ... this concupiscence is always in us; therefore the love of God is never in us, except in so far as grace has given us a beginning of it .... this life is a life of cure from sin; it is not a life of sinlessness, as if the cure were finished and health had been recovered. The church is an inn and an infirmary for the sick and for convalescents. Heaven, however, is the palace where the whole and the righteous live.'[86]

---

86 *Lectures on Romans*. Library of Christian Classics, Volume XV, pp. 127, 128, 129, 130.

Faith, Freedom, Works and Law

What is the relationship between works, law and sanctification? For the believer the works done are works done in faith, with no thought of works being done at all, and certainly not for merit. Merit is not a New Testament word. 'Obedience' and 'following' are New Testament words. Above all 'freedom' is a New Testament word. Such freedom as the Christian knows is found in Jesus Christ and not in any adherence to an obedience-cult, where adherence to the letter is more important than faith in the Lord. But faith is not quiescent. One does not escape the demands of worldly living because one has faith. Now for the first time one comes to see what the demands of living in the world really mean. For faith, sanctification does not mean removal from the world but progress and conflict within it. We are sanctified in our human nature. There is no other for us. We do deeds. The deeds we do are the deeds of faith. The moralist may do the same deeds without faith. The deeds the believer does may appear to be the same deeds, but because faith is present they are different deeds. It is faith that makes the difference. Their influence in the world may be the same as the deeds not done in faith. We must be content.

The deeds of faith are done within the world. The locus of the process called sanctification is world. There is to be no escapism from world. In the rough and tumble of daily existence, in an impersonal, sometimes arid, sometimes hostile atmosphere, there is the scene for the manifestation of faith. As sanctification is the affair of this life and not of one beyond, so also it is an affair for this world and not for another. The one who is sanctified is sanctified here and now or nowhere and never, which means not at all. We do not escape the world by physical retreat, or by denying we are in it. There is to be no creation of an artificial world in which we may be sanctified. Faith connects God with life in its multitudinous aspects.

The Pauline word is appropriate, '... let every one lead the life which the Lord has assigned to him, and in which God has called

Justification by Grace Through Faith 125

him. This is my rule in all the churches,' *I Corinthians.* 7:17. Faith does not require us to create the world in which we shall manifest it. That is a work which would destroy the faith. Our world is given to us and in it we find the vocation of the Christian as faith is applied to the tasks which that world presents for us.

The deeds of faith are deeds performed in the liberty of sonship. That is what distinguishes them from works. The creation of a set of rules, necessary as it may appear for the regulation of the life of faith, is the first step for the destruction of the liberty of the gospel. Since rules are made to be followed and pressure is brought to bear to see that the purpose for which they were made is not unfulfilled, the fulfillment of the rules may emerge as more important than the faith which the formulation of the rules was created to safeguard. Then faith gets forgotten. It happened at Galatia. It happened during the Middle Ages. It has happened since.

Emil Brunner criticises the Reformed church for the introduction of the *usus tertius legis,* 'the 'third use of the law'. The function of the law here proposed is to place restraint upon the man of faith, lest he be released from all restraint. This he calls the 'reintroduction of the law by the back door'.[87] Brunner calls it 'moralism' since it reintroduces the law to provide restraint, fearing that faith in Jesus Christ as Lord is not sufficient. One cannot break free from general rules of obligation. So a new legalism results, a kind of Christian Pharisaism 'which ever and again sacrifices the spontaneity of love to legalistic rule of thumb and leaves in practice hardly any room for the embodiment of the creative, intuitive and unpharisaic freedom of God's children'.[88] It is a repetition of the relapse of the Galatians, who rejected life in the Spirit with its freedom, to whom Paul said, 'But if you are led by the spirit, you are not under the law. *Galatians* 5:18. The man who does not

---

87 Emil Brunner, *The Christian Doctrine of The Church, Faith, and the Consummation.* Dogmatics: Vol. III, translated by David Cairns. Philadelphia: The Westminster Press, 1962, p. 300.
88 Ibid., p. 301.

understand himself in the light of God's self-bestowing love knows of no higher authority than the law.[89]

But it often happens that the attempt to restrain faith destroys it. Love is greater than law; and the man who does not yet understand the absolute demands and the freedom of love for Christ can find no higher authority than that of law. To know Jesus Christ is to know the constraint of the absolute. That is true freedom: to know the demand that invites imagination, and the imaginative fulfillment of that demand. It is to be more conscious of Jesus Christ than of the constraint.

When the letter is emphasised and the spirit forgotten, relationship with God is replaced by relation to an external code. Legalism is the attempted approach to God via law. Any law! To do something to gain God's favour, something, anything — that is legalism. A devotion to law for the sake of merit is in no way consonant with faith.

This is the point of Paul's reference to Abraham. Even if Abraham were one of the most godly men of his age, that mattered nothing. God need not have chosen him. God did not make the promise to him on the basis of any goodness. (Cf. *Romans* 4:2–5 where Paul contrasts the way of faith and the way of works.)

> 'For if Abraham were justified by works, he hath whereof to glory, but not before God. For what saith the scripture? Abraham believed God, and it was counted to him for righteousness. Now to him that worketh is the reward not reckoned of grace, but of debt. But to him that worketh not, but believeth on him that justifieth the ungodly, his faith is counted for righteousness.'

Whatever works Abraham could claim made no difference to his relation to God. No work of man can put God in his debt or be made the basis of the fulfilment of God's promises. The payment of a debt and the bestowal of a gift are two completely different acts, and call for two completely differing responses.

---

89 Ibid.

If we present someone with something they do not want and have not asked for it is obviously unwelcome. It does not help that we offer a lot. It is not a question of quantity. The situation is unchanged whatever quantity we offer of something that is not wanted. If they do not want what we offer the more we give the worse is the situation. The more that is offered the worse it becomes — until there may be a breaking point. That is what happened with Paul and with Luther. They fulfilled all the obligations they knew and found no peace with God. They multiplied works. But they achieved no acceptance. That is why Paul condemned legalism as an impossible system. Explicitly he stated that the way of law requires total obedience. Every last precept must be followed. It is all or nothing. The alternatives are either complete obedience or condemnation. But this is impossible, and its impossibility shows the futility of the way of law as a way of approach to God. Since what we have to offer, in Pauline terms the works of law, is not acceptable, it does not matter how much we offer: zeal that knows no respite, tears that forever flow, flagellations that never cease, prayers that never end, multiplied deeds of charity. 'All for sin could not atone. Thou must save and thou alone.' So in *Galatians* 3:10,11 Paul affirms:

> 'For all who rely on works are under a curse; for it is written, 'Cursed be every one who does not abide by all things written in the book of the law, and do them.' Now it is evident that no man is justified before God by the law: for 'He who through faith is righteous shall live'.

Thus if there is a way to be found to God it will be the antithesis of law. In Jesus Christ that way has been found, 'But now the righteousness of God has been manifested apart from law. *Romans*. 3:21. What is meant by law here is a way of approach to God via the performance of the deeds of law, without the presence of faith. This usage of the term 'law' has been defined as 'divine law viewed as a purely legalistic system made up of statutes of the basis of obedience or disobedience to which it justifies or condemns.[90] There was no guarantee of freedom from sin under this way. In fact the law seemed to gain in authority every time it was broken. Man's impotence in face of it, his indwelling sin dominating him, gave to the law the power of a tyrant. As long as sin is present, the power of the law is present and law condemns. When sin is removed the sting is drawn from the law. And when the sin is removed, the law ceases to be a way of life, *Romans* 8:3,4.

> 'For what the law could not do, in that it was weak through the flesh, God sending his own son in the likeness of sinful flesh, and for sin, condemned sin in the flesh: that the righteousness of the law might be fulfilled in us, who walk not after the flesh, but after the Spirit'

That new way of life is described by the expression 'under grace'. So Paul asserts, 'Ye are not under law but under grace.' *Romans* 6:14. And as usual he meant what he said. The statement is made, interestingly enough, in connection with another, 'for sin shall not have dominion over you', which precedes. This connection the legalist always misses. To be free from the dominion of sin you must repudiate law. If it is freedom from sin that we quest, 'under law' must be rejected for 'under grace'. The legalist says that the only way there is freedom from the dominion of sin is by putting myself 'under law'. The antithesis could not have been more sharply drawn as it has been in this verse. We may take our choice. 'Under grace', the way of law is over and done with once and for all. Through grace we see that adherence to law any law, divinely given or humanly framed, majestic or trite, is a blind alley if peace with God and sanctification of life is sought. The rejection of law at this essential point is our only shield against antinomianism, as it is our only shield against legalism. For the despair that ensues from the attempt to keep law may easily lead to an accommodation of its requirements and to a casuistry that is more concerned about avoiding the injunction than in following it.

---

90 Burton. *Commentary on Galatians*, p. 457.

It is in the context of an experienced grace, and a continuing faith, which is to say, in the context of relationship with God that the 'works' of the Christian are done. Since they are spontaneous they do not occupy the foreground of attention. For one who really has faith, the obedience which the discipleship requires at this point is forthcoming. It is the fruit and the evidence of the discipleship. And the discipleship is often expressed in unpredictable ways, as new demands are made upon one's obedience. It is the unpredictability of the demand that the legalist cannot stand. He must know all and everything now. The trust that is absolute requires no assurances for the future, except that which is given by the present relationship.

Sanctification thus has its eschatological aspect. The believer must wage the warfare against sin, the flesh and the devil. He knows both that the victory has already been won, as well as he knows that the victory is not yet. In Christ sin has been judged, and thus vanquished. At the parousia it will be finally obliterated. While living between the times, the believer enters into the victory of the former, and anticipates the victory of the latter. Christ has conquered, and will conquer. The believer shares in one victory and anticipates the other. Between the cross and the eschaton the believer demonstrates the reality of that conquest.

The way of faith is a way of freedom. To abandon faith for law is to abandon freedom for bondage. One cannot add law to Gospel and hope that benefit will ensue. A decided choice between the two must be made. That is the point of Paul's allegory of Sarah and Hagar, with the command he draws from it: 'Cast out the slave and her son; for the son of the slave shall not inherit with the son of the free woman,' *Galatians* 4:30.

The fifth chapter of *Galatians* continues the theme of the relationship between the way of law and the way of grace. The first verse bases the admonition to stand in freedom upon the accomplished fact that Christ has set us free. Jesus has won the freedom. The believer is to stand fast in that which has been won. The implication is that to fail in maintaining freedom is to deny the work of Christ. This statement links the exposition that follows to the analogy. If circumcision, that is, any work of law, and hence law as a way of salvation, be accepted, the freedom ensuing to the believer by the accomplished fact of Jesus Christ is forfeited; moreover the whole law, not simply one precept of it has to be fulfilled. Such a one 'is bound to keep the whole law'. 'You are severed from Christ, you who would be justified by the law;' you have fallen away from grace, verses 3,4. The fourth verse is worthy of more attention. An article precedes 'grace' but is absent before 'law'. You who would be justified by way of law, through adherence to law, who seek the legalistic way, you are separated from that grace which has been made known in Jesus Christ. The way of law, which can have any law as its focus of interest, effectively nullifies the grace of God, decisively manifest in Jesus Christ. A fall has taken place: 'you have fallen away from grace' verse 4. A fall is a movement to a state where relation to God is repudiated: the fall, in this context, is the repudiation of Christ. The eschatological note enters in the fifth verse: 'For we through the spirit wait for the hope of righteousness by faith. Here Paul suggests that the future to the believer is open. To the recipient of grace the future is filled with hope. The realisation of the hope will be of righteousness not in the law (*dikaiosunes* not *en nomoi*). The present is a present of hope. It is a present of hope in faith. The hope of the Christian is based upon faith. Remove the faith, and the hope vanishes. Then the future becomes empty. Justification leads to hope. This is evident in the confidence that characterises the present. The anticipated future is present in faith. It is an eschatological present.

In the sixth verse Paul answers the question, 'What matters?' In short his answer is 'Nothing matters but faith working through love' (*pistis di' agapes energoumene*). This passage is of particular interest since it is the only place in the Pauline writings where faith and love are brought together in this way. The ethic that is involved here is a very simple one in its most fundamental statement. Faith begets love and through love becomes operative in conduct. The moral dynamic of the believer's life is to be found in faith. The work which faith manifests is the work of love. Freedom from law leads neither to inaction nor does it leave life without moral incentive. Faith is a working thing, 'a busy, living, active faith' (Luther), which manifests itself. Faith expresses itself. Faith is not an introversive phenomenon. Faith does not need completion, as if it lacked something which could be supplied by works of love. It is not that faith needs to be formed by love, to be *fides formata caritate*. Faith, complete in itself, expresses itself in activity, the activity of love. Apart from such faith, nothing matters. That is what the first part of the verse says. This verse makes quite explicit the antithesis between the way of faith and the way of works, the way of law. 'It would be well if we had the courage to bring all our ecclesiastical and theological differences into the searching light of this verse. If 'circumcision' is to be regarded as in effect covering everything in religion that is not directly related with faith and love, it covers many many things that we make a great bother about in Church circles.[91]

When we said, as we did above, that the works of the Christian are performed in the context of faith, of experienced grace, the intention was to say that those works are quite unacceptable to God without the faith that provided the context. Whatever we do is always imperfect. Our works are the works of the guilty. They are the works of the sinner, albeit the justified sinner. The works are only acceptable as the sinner is justified. The works are not acceptable in themselves. The believer, as the one of faith and so in relation to God, is accepted and not rejected. What the believer does, imperfect as it may be, is accepted and not rejected. The works of the regenerate do not justify them. Acceptable good works are present only as God himself is present.

JAMES AND PAUL ON WORKS AND FAITH

The first impression many people get on reading *James* alongside of Paul is that in speaking of 'faith' and 'works' Paul, with

---

91 John. A. Allen, *Galatians*, London: S. C. M. Press, 1964, p. 79.

emphasis on faith only, is deliberately contradicted by James who calls for works as well as faith and as evidence for it. Both quote *Genesis* 15:6, 'Abraham believed God, and it was reckoned unto him for righteousness' but go on to draw different conclusions from the passage. It helps if we think of James as not making a reply to Paul's teaching. Very probably James is protesting against a misunderstanding or even a deliberate perversion of Paul's teaching. This is what *James* says in the passage in question.

> What doth it profit, my brethren, though a man say he hath faith, and have not works? Can faith save him? If a brother or sister be naked and destitute of daily food, And one of you say unto them Depart in peace, be ye warmed and filled, nevertheless ye give them not the things that are needful to the body; what doth it profit? Even so faith, if it hath not works, is dead, being alone *(James* 2:14–17).

A professed faith without corresponding works is worthless. No one is profited if, being poor, he be told to be clothed without practical help being given. Just so faith without works is dead. It is not real faith that finds no expression in works. The devils shudder and they have faith. In Abraham's case his willingness to offer Isaac was a demonstration of the genuineness of the faith through which righteousness was imputed. In Rahab's case she acted quickly when she received the messengers. Faith without works is dead.

Things become clear if we examine the respective meanings these two writers give to the key terms, which both of them use.

James makes reference to devils who tremble as they believe. They give assent and are afraid for what they believe. So for *James* faith means assent, assent to the doctrines of Christianity. It is good to believe, give assent to the proposition, that God is one (verse 19). But intellectual assent is insufficient for God's approval. Nor does genuine faith cause one to shudder in fear before God. A faith that is merely an expression of belief is useless, unless supported by good works. Christian acts are the necessary complement of Christian faith. ' ... the writer sharply controverts a faith which is little more

Justification by Grace Through Faith

than the assent to a creed (2:19), a faith which need not have any relation to conduct at all.[92]

Paul's faith is an attitude of self abandonment, and confidence. It is a new orientation of life with Christ at the centre, personal trust and surrender, a deep, intimate personal relationship, not the belief of James. Paul would have denied that James' faith could save.

Works for *James* are the fruits of faith. He is clearly speaking of acts of Christian love which when done show that the faith is genuine. They are evidence for faith. So if for 'evidence' we substitute 'fruit' we shall not go far wrong. They are evidence of faith, the fruit of faith. So they are as such not the means of obtaining God's favour. Faith is not genuine if it is barren. It is only genuine if it leads to fruitage in good deeds. *James*' '*works*' are then equivalent to Paul's 'fruits' They indicate a genuine faith. As for Paul, so for James they are not *erga nomou* 'meritorious deeds of legal obedience. They do not save, 'a man is judged by faith apart from works of the law,' *Romans* 3:28. Paul also recognised that true faith issues in action, e.g. *Galatians* 5:6 where he writes of the 'faith which worketh by love'. There are other New Testament passages maintaining a similar connection between faith and good works, e.g. *Ephesians*. 2:10: 'created in Christ Jesus unto good works'; *Titus* 3:8 '... they which have believed in God be careful to maintain good works'. To speak of such good works for Paul is not legalism. Nor is it to repudiate the proper function of law. Rather 'we establish the law'. *Romans* 3:31.

We turn now to the term 'justified'. For Paul it means the acceptance of the sinner in God's sight. For James, it means the approval received by man from God. Paul says Abraham was justified when he believed God. *Romans* 4:3, *Galatians* 3:6. This is in reference to the original promise made to Abraham, quoted from Gen. 15:6 'And he believed in the Lord; and he counted it to him for righteousness, i.e. before Isaac was born.

---

92 H. A. A. Kennedy, *The Theology of the Epistles*. London: Duckworth, 1919, p. 227.

James is speaking of the proof Abraham gave that the faith which resulted in God's imputing of righteousness was genuine faith. It led to Abraham's willingness to offer his son. He is not defining the method of justification, but showing that Abraham's faith was proved to be genuine by what he did. James stresses conduct. For James, conduct is threefourths of life. For Paul the emphasis is on faith as means of acceptance.

XIII ALL IS OF GOD

Faith and church

The church is the community of shared faith. The presence of faith in the life of the one who believes provides a point of contact with the other believers who have come to know faith. Thus there is the opportunity for fellowship not before possible. The church is the community of faith. It is the 'communion of saints'. It is the communion between the kind of persons who are described by the New Testament term *hagios*. The church is thus not an exhibition of saints having arrived. Rather it is the place where the believer bears witness to his faith in Jesus Christ, and where that faith is nurtured by the very act of witness. It is the place where those who believe are to be found, These are in the state of progress, which is sanctification.

Thus the activities of the church are related to the event of faith. For apart from this act of faith, there would be no church. Intrinsic to the church's life have been certain fundamental acts: those of preaching, participating in the liturgy and the sacraments, of declaring the meaning of the church's life in creed and theology. When the doctrine of the church is considered, these themes also call for consideration. They are aspects of ecclesiology, the doctrine of the church. They find their centre in the fact of faith. Preaching is a means of nurturing faith, as in the act of declaring 'the word' witness is borne to the basic fact of faith, Jesus Christ. The character of the community is determined by the act of Jesus Christ. The community remembers and declares this act of Jesus Christ. For this act requires to be expounded for faith to be nurtured. The church preaches about many things but what is of primary importance is that the preaching be related to the Christ event.

Creeds and dogmas are expositions of faith. Theology differs from speculation in that it is based upon the given fact of faith. It, in its way, by pointing to the reasonableness of faith, shows that reason may be fulfilled and not violated in the understanding of faith. The sacraments are the visible witness to faith. Liturgy is an attempt to express faith and hence to assist in the nurturing and the maturing of faith. Faith thus finds expression is many different ways: the many-sidedness of the expression of faith corresponds to the many-sidedness of the life of the mature Christian.

The need to express faith in order to nurture it bears witness to the character of faith as event. Faith is living only as it expresses itself in the life of the believer and of the believing community. The distinctiveness of the church does not therefore lie in its having attained. For to have attained would make the assistances to faith unnecessary. The saints still need to have their faith nurtured within the church. The church is a convalescent home, not a showcase of perfection.

The church exists within world. Christianity is a worldaffirming religion. However, while the distinction between the church and world cannot be radicalised, it cannot, at the other extreme, be denied. Church is distinct from world but church exists within world. The world is the sphere of faith, and church is in world. The church is not that particular piece of world which has now ceased to be world because it has become 'sanctified'.

> 'This tendency not to allow the world to be the sphere of faith, but to mark off a special sphere from the world as the sphere of the church and of faith — that is, the tendency to sanctify a piece of the world — leads to the opposite danger, that of the holy being made worldly. We might put it in a sentence: to clericalise the world is just a special form of secularising the church.'[93]

---

93   Gerhard Ebeling, *op. cit.* p. 156.

'All is of God'

We shall end where we began, by stressing the fact that all is of God. The way of life the Christian lives is that of holiness. God is holy. Man's holiness is derivative from God. It is God who sanctifies. 'I am the Lord which sanctify you' *Leviticus* 20:8. 'The very God of peace sanctify you wholly' *I Thessalonians* 5:23. It is God's name, that is he himself, who is sanctified among his people.

The primary fact is that God is holy. This is a constant theme in the Old Testament. 'Holy is He', 'For the Lord our God is holy' *Psalm* 99:3,5. 'Ye shall be holy for I the Lord your God am holy' *Leviticus* 19:2. A thing or a person is holy because consecrated to God. The basic meaning of the term *qadosh* is that of separation, that which is separated, cut off from a profane and set apart for a holy use. The idea of power is also associated with the term. Sometimes the person is spoken of as separate. That one is holy. The Hebrew root has a rich connotation. 'The same root successively denotes a state and an action, the action suffered or produced, and the subject or object of that action.'[94]

For the Old Testament holiness has to do with relationship to the covenant, that is relationship to the God of the covenant. Israel is holy because of its relationship to God, because it is separated to him. 'Yahweh is the holy one of Israel not because he is consecrated to Israel but because he has consecrated Israel to himself, and Israel itself is holy only because of this consecration to Yahweh.'[95] Man is holy only in relation to God, through the covenant. God is holy in himself. This means that God can manifest his holiness in independence of those with whom he is in relationship through the covenant. Moreover, if men break the covenant God still remains holy. A perversion of this relationship aspect was possible. If an object were regarded as holy and the relationship to God was

---
94   Edmond Jacob, pp. cit., p. 87.
95   Ibid., p. 89.

forgotten it could be thought of as being intrinsically holy. But the Old Testament regards things and persons as holy only as they are in relation to God, and never in themselves.

This materialisation of holiness led to its being regarded as a state. But things are not holy in themselves. They are not holy by nature. They become holy. That is holy which is in relation to God. The ground has become holy because God is present:

> And when the Lord saw that he turned aside to see, God called unto him from out of the midst of the bush and said, Moses, Moses. And he said, Here am I. And he said, Draw not nigh hither: put off thy shoes from off thy feet, for the place whereon thou standest is holy ground. *Exodus* 3:4–5.

Those objects which have to do with the worship of God are holy as they are used in the service of God and so are brought into relation with God. So the ark is holy. The vessels of the temple are holy. *II Chronicles* 35:3. *I Kings* 8:4 where the ark and the temple vessels are called 'holy': 'the holy ark', 'the holy vessels'.

The New Testament conception is similar. It is God who sanctifies. God is the proper subject of sanctification. Christ sanctifies, in that he is equal with God. So e.g. 'Christ loved the church and gave himself up for her, that he might sanctify her' *Ephesians* 5:25; 'I consecrate myself that they also may be consecrated in truth' 17:19. The Holy Spirit is the source of sanctification. The Spirit is holy, and the work of the Spirit is sanctification. The 'spiritual' man is the one in whom the Spirit is dominant. He it is who, having been justified, now continues in the Godgiven faith. 'God chose you from the beginning to be saved through sanctification by the spirit' *II Thessalonians* 2:13. The New Testament speaks of holiness as the result of the activity of God and in terms of relationship with God. Since the decisive act of God has been made in Jesus Christ, and since the presence of God subsequent to the human presence of God among men in Jesus Christ has assumed a yet different form, God is spoken of in the New Testament as Father, Son and Spirit. The passages where this is done are familiar e.g. II *Corinthians*

Justification by Grace Through Faith

12:14: 'The grace of the Lord Jesus Christ, and the love of God, and the communion of the Holy Ghost, be with you all. Amen.'

The sanctification of the believer is traced to Christ and his work. It is God who sanctifies. The first letter to the Corinthians is addressed to 'those sanctified in Christ Jesus. *I Corinthians* 1:2. Similarly it is stated, 'you were sanctified ... in the name of the Lord Jesus Christ and in the Spirit of our God' 6:11. So deeprooted is this conviction that man's sanctification is dependent and derived that it can be traced to the eternal purpose of God. Man is elected to be sanctified by God, 'chosen and destined by God the Father and sanctified by the Spirit for obedience to Jesus Christ' *I Peter* 1:2. To this may be compared the Pauline word, 'God chose you ... unto salvation in sanctification of the Spirit ... to the obtaining of the glory of our Lord Jesus Christ' *II Thessalonians* 2:13. It was God's initial purpose to make faith possible. This has been accomplished in Jesus Christ, and mediated through the Spirit.

Faith is of God. Sanctification is of God.

Assurance

The decisive work has been done in Jesus Christ. We cannot gain anything by our works. 'God does not judge us according to what we achieve but suffers us to serve him for Christ's sake.... Trust that our obedience will please our Father no matter how small it is. (Calvin). Many people who pray and fast, lead a good life before their fellows, when they are asked whether they are certain that what they do pleases God will say that they are not sure.

Indeed the medieval church regarded such uncertainty as a healthy discipline; it tended to look suspiciously on 'joy and peace in believing' (cf. *Romans* 15:13) as a form of presumption. As Pope Gregory put it with the bland arrogance of all paternalism, *Sancta ecclesia fidelibus suis ... spem miscet et metum* (Holy Church mingles hope and fear for her faithful children.) Replying to one of the ladies-in-waiting at the imperial court, who had written to him for assurance, the great pope replied: *secura de peccatis tuis fieri non debes* (thou shouldst not become easy in mind about thy sins) ....

the whole degrading trade in indulgences which became a moral outrage in the early sixteenth century, shows that the scrupulous Catholic did not know and might not know on what terms he stood, so to speak, with God. Luther felt that he must know.'[96]

Assurance is based on the personal nature of the grace of God, the mercy which one may encounter in Jesus Christ. Grace is not an ontological substance infused into one below the level of consciousness, a 'quasi-physical force', 'an ineffable divine energy … impinging on the soul. Grace is God's forgiving love which accepts the sinner and restores him to relationship to himself. Grace is 'the personal mercy of God which we encounter in Christ', 'the Father's saving will', 'the free active love of God to sinners.'[97] This grace makes possible, indeed inevitable, the assurance of the believer.

---

[96] J.S. Whale, *The Protestant Tradition.* Cambridge: Cambridge University Press, 1955, p. 67.
[97] H. R. Mackintosh, *op. cit.*, pp. 143-144, 149.

www.ingramcontent.com/pod-product-compliance
Lightning Source LLC
Chambersburg PA
CBHW030046100426
42734CB00036B/373